J. Van Lindley

His Ancestors, Life, and Legacy

Joseph C. Carlin

J. Van Lindley

Copyright © 2011 by Joseph C. Carlin

Dedications

Inspiration – To Lindley Kirksey Young and John Van Lindley III, whose passion to find out more about their family, inspired completion of this book.

Honor - To my wife Shirley Stovall Carlin and her mother Pearl Lindley Sykes. They are among the many Lindley descended women who left behind the family's last name, but kept a passionate attachment alive, feeding us family stories along with love and great Southern cooking.

Legacy - To my sons J.P. Carlin and David Sykes Carlin, and their many cousins, so that the 150 years that separate them from their 2nd Great Grandfather, John Van Mons Lindley, may evaporate, bringing his presence into their hearts and thoughts on a daily basis.

Acknowledgments

This book reached completion because of the unflagging and enthusiastic support of my wife, Shirley Stovall Carlin, the great-grand daughter of J. Van Lindley. Her cousins Lindley Kirksey Young and John Van Lindley III also provided a substantial contribution by commissioning Ridley Smith to research the Lindley family, then generously sharing the results. Ridley's research, along with my previous research, formed the basis for the structure of this book.

I would like to thank the many county staff, archivists and librarians at each of the wonderfully maintained facilities where I performed my research within North Carolina (NC): Alamance County Library and Register of Deeds, Chatham County Library and Register of Deeds, Forsyth County Register of Deeds, Guilford College Archives, Guilford County Register of Deeds, Greensboro Historical Museum Archives, Greensboro Library, Harnett County Library and Register of Deeds, Moore County Library and Register of Deeds, NC State Archives, Orange County Library and Register of Deeds, University of NC (UNC) at Chapel Hill Libraries, UNC-Greensboro Library, and Wake County's Olivia Raney Local History Library.

In particular, I would like to thank Elizabeth (Liz) P. Cook, Archives Associate at Guilford College, who went well above and beyond my expectations in finding every Lindley connection to the college; Steve Catlett, the Greensboro Historical Museum Archivist; and Audrey Moriarity, Executive Director of the Tufts Archive in Pinehurst, NC.

Finally, I would like to thank those who helped me get to the finished product - Rob and Marsha Moore, cousins who contributed by reading the text, making suggestions, and asking good questions that prompted me to find the answers, and my father, Paul N. Carlin, who was instrumental in helping me work through designing the cover.

Preface

This book began with my personal interest in genealogy. I connected over 20,000 individuals related to my wife and myself using Family Tree Maker software. The software made it easy because I built on the efforts of others by importing and merging their databases. I then proceeded to check and augment the information they provided using online research tools. It wasn't long before I had lots of information about the ancestors of my wife and our sons, the Lindley family. I had so much information that I wondered about the best way to share what I had learned.

Meanwhile, several of my wife's cousins had been doing research on J. Van Lindley and shared their information with me – four large binders of material. One of these cousins was named John Van Lindley III. He was a very private person and a recluse by nature. I never met him in person, but we talked on the telephone and mailed information back and forth for a few years before he died. As I sat in relative obscurity at his funeral in May of 2009, I was moved by the shortness of time that we each have on earth. I decided to take the next step and create a book out of our material.

Naivety can be a good friend, as I didn't know much effort lay in front of me. The initial writing was completed nine months later. Shirley's cousins Rob and Marsha Moore joined me in reading through the first half of the book. As we all read aloud and asked questions, I recognized the need for thoroughly scouring all available research facilities. That led to trips to the libraries and register of deeds offices for many counties in NC: Alamance, Chatham, Guilford, Harnett, Moore, Orange and Wake. This was supplemented by trips to the University of North Carolina, NC State Archives, Pinehurst Archives, Greensboro Historical Society, and Guilford College. I also spent many weeks performing online searches that led to a treasure trove of Google Books that are out of print, but available to read online or download for later reference.

To really understand the Lindley men, I felt it was necessary to collect and analyze available land and business transactions. As a former business executive, my interest was in how
these men made a living and took advantage of opportunities. I
researched and recorded every known real estate transaction for
the subjects of this book, then created databases of hundreds of
real estate transactions, along with their recorded values to
understand the economic impact of their decisions and the
extent of their wealth. I also input the land dimensions from
over 100 land transactions into a specialized software program
to identify and re-create graphically the dimensions of the land
that these men owned. The results of these studies helped in
understanding what was important to these men from a business perspective.

While the library and onsite research was extensive and
the primary research complex, my emphasis in the presentation
of the material has been to simplify. For example, several wills
are presented word-for-word, but then summarized and the
sections on the Civil War and J. Van Lindley's European trip are
presented in outline form. The point of this approach is to allow
the reader to be presented with a simplified overview instead of
extensive detail. This was also necessary in order to cover 300
years of activity within an easily readable number of pages.

The book that results from all of these efforts is interesting in recognizing that history is an accumulation of the personal lives of those living at the time. The lives of these men touch
events known to all students of American History like the early
settling of Pennsylvania, the migration over the Great Philadelphia Wagon Road, the War of the Regulators in North Carolina,
the Revolutionary War, the Underground Railroad, the Civil
War, the Industrial Revolution and the advent of trains and
automobiles. This book is a guided trip through the history of
one thin line of related men - sons following in the footsteps of
their fathers for 8 generations. Each man's life represents a
thread in the fabric of United States history as: the Quakers
sought freedom and justice; pioneers bought and cleared land in
Pennsylvania, North Carolina and Indiana; farmers planted and
harvested crops year after year; and especially as these early

businessmen led the way in developing the fruit tree industry in the southeastern United States.

Finally, I have a few comments for the reader about documentation and quotes within the book. First, the focus of this book is on a factual presentation of available information about the Lindley family. Citations are used throughout to identify the source for each fact within the book. For example, the first citation is for a source on the origin of the Lindley family name and looks like this: (Dictionary of American Family Names). The book reference can be found in alphabetical order in the bibliography at the end of the book. Where available, page references are incorporated into the citation. This approach, a divergence from most scholarly works, eliminates the unnecessary duplication of the same information into over 100 footnotes. Second, because of the emphasis on factual sources, very little family tradition (stories handed down from generation to generation) has been included, but where it has been it is so noted. Third, many of the quotes come from transcriptions of source documents and contain misspellings, especially the wills. These misspellings are intentionally presented and only occasionally corrected. They give the reader insight into the level of education, which was low, for people during these early periods in American history.

Since this book can only present a fraction of the information available, if you have any interest in further exploring the material in this book or would like to schedule a reading, presentation or discussion, please feel free to contact me by email at: jccarlin@mac.com.

My hope is that you enjoy reading as much as I enjoyed researching and writing this book.

Table of Contents

List of Illustrations

Introduction

Who was J. Van Lindley?

John Van Mons Lindley, who preferred to be called J. Van Lindley, was a quiet man with a strikingly different name. He was a Quaker who fought in the Civil War. He was a Pomologist (fruit tree grower) by family tradition and personal passion. He was one of the early Nurserymen in North Carolina and likely had the largest nursery operation in the then known world with 1.5 million plants and a peach orchard with rows of trees a mile and a half long. He was an ardent entrepreneur who started many companies, including a Terra Cotta manufacturing company and an insurance company that became Jefferson-Pilot Life Insurance Company. He served on the Board of Directors for many companies and was a trustee of Guilford College for 33 years. At his own expense, he built an elementary school and donated it to Guilford County. He was President of many state and national associations and organizations. He traveled across the western United States and throughout Europe and the Middle East. These were many of his accomplishments.

Who was this humble Quaker farmer that became such a successful businessman? What type of man was he? From where did he and his family originate? What were their beliefs? Did others admire them? How did others view him personally? Was he loud, brash and hard driving? Was he ruthless, focused and driven? Was he bitter following the Civil War? How did he handle tragedy? How did he handle success? How did he treat his family and others?

This book explores these questions. It is divided into five parts:

Introduction: This section includes a short introduction and insight into the origin of the family
name.

Early and then Immediate Ancestors: The interesting lives of J. Van Lindley's ancestors are explored.

J. Van Lindley: His life is explained in detail, based
upon available historical facts and supplemented
with family histories.

Legacy: J. Van Lindley left a large legacy, which
spread, to many within his family and throughout
his community of Greensboro and, through his
companies, across the United States for many
years following his death.

The story of J. Van Lindley began with his English ancestors, who migrated to Ireland and then to America in search of
religious freedom and economic opportunity. Their story is the
story of the settling and growth of first the Colonies of America
and then the United States of America. Like his ancestors, J.
Van Lindley became a great example of a successful American
during the 19th and early 20th Century.

His life of great achievement did not come early, easily, or
without great effort. As a young man, he survived the loss of his
mother and had only one semester of formal schooling. He saw
the horrors of the Civil War first hand and returned to find his
hometown of Greensboro in ruin and his father deeply in debt.
He also watched his first wife die within a year of their marriage
and then, with his second wife, they lost a child that died before
the age of two. Finally, he watched his fellow Southerners
struggle for 40 years following the Civil War.

J. Van Lindley survived tragedy and disappointment. He
carried on the strong Quaker faith passed down to him by six
previous generations of believers, counting his early relatives
among the faith's earliest believers. His faith was also inter-
twined with strong family connections from several generations
of large Quaker farming families that intermarried. He learned
his profession working alongside his father Joshua Lindley, a

passionate Pomologist, who was recognized as one of the fathers of fruit growing in both North Carolina and Indiana.

This short summary gives a thumbnail sketch of the life of J. Van Lindley and his ancestors. As the rest of the pages of this book unfold, we will witness the progress of the Quaker religion from its infancy down through seven generations and across three countries. We also see a family, which was integrally woven into three pioneer migrations that defined the events of early America. The progress of the Lindley family down through time, and their impact on the exceptional man that J. Van Lindley became, demonstrate clearly that each of us as individuals are created, shaped and formed by our ancestors, our world, and the change each of us brings to the world.

Origin of the Lindley Name

The last name of Lindley comes from an Old English name derived from two elements: the first is Lin which means "flax" or Lind which means "lime tree" and the second is Leah which means "wooded," "woodland clearing" or "glade" (Dictionary of American Family Names). Other possible origins include the name coming from Saxon for "flax meadow" or Germanic with the word "lind" denoting an area of "linden" (or lime) trees (Wikipedia).

The name may have originated in one of five places in England:

The first is in North Yorkshire, about two miles from the town of Otley.

The second is in West Yorkshire where the town of Lindley is a suburb of Huddersfield and lies two miles northwest of Huddersfield's town center.

The third is the town of Linley in Shropshire.

Fourth, the name Linley also shows up in roads and streets in Wiltshire (Dictionary of American Family Names).

The final possible origin comes from the name for
the specific town mentioned in Cheshire, England
named "Lindenlea" where the oldest ancestor
commonly recognized by most genealogists was
born.

Since many surnames were developed from medieval occupations, the linen connection is worth understanding. Linen is
a product of the flax plant, whose fibers have been used as long
as wool fibers to make clothing. The English and Normans of the
Middle Ages grew the plants, pulled them out by the roots and
then processed them by separating out the seeds, drying the
plants and then beating out the woody tissue to pull out the
precious fibers. The fibers were subsequently spun into thread
using, with a few adjustments, the same loom as for wool.

The name Lindley means that these individuals either
owned or lived close to a field of flax. It is an ancient name as
there was a Godwin de Linacra as far back as 1086, the year in
which William the Conqueror took his Doomsday Survey
(Dolan).

For a family that later became well known for several
generations as leading landowners, farmers and Pomologists,
coming from a country with rich soil and having a name derived
from land ownership or a useful plant seems appropriate.

Early Ancestors

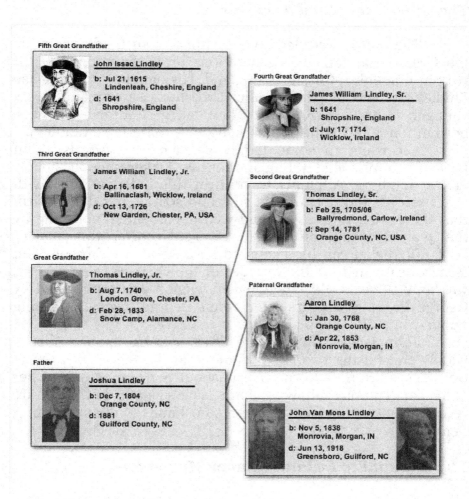

Fifth Great Grandfather

John Issac Lindley

b: Jul 21, 1615
   Lindenleah, Cheshire, England
d: 1641
   Shropshire, England

Fourth Great Grandfather

James William Lindley, Sr.

b: 1641
   Shropshire, England
d: July 17, 1714
   Wicklow, Ireland

Third Great Grandfather

James William Lindley, Jr.

b: Apr 16, 1681
   Ballinaclash, Wicklow, Ireland
d: Oct 13, 1726
   New Garden, Chester, PA, USA

Second Great Grandfather

Thomas Lindley, Sr.

b: Feb 25, 1705/06
   Ballyredmond, Carlow, Ireland
d: Sep 14, 1781
   Orange County, NC, USA

Great Grandfather

Thomas Lindley, Jr.

b: Aug 7, 1740
   London Grove, Chester, PA
d: Feb 28, 1833
   Snow Camp, Alamance, NC

Paternal Grandfather

Aaron Lindley

b: Jan 30, 1768
   Orange County, NC
d: Apr 22, 1853
   Monrovia, Morgan, IN

Father

Joshua Lindley

b: Dec 7, 1804
   Orange County, NC
d: 1881
   Guilford County, NC

John Van Mons Lindley

b: Nov 5, 1838
   Monrovia, Morgan, IN
d: Jun 13, 1918
   Greensboro, Guilford, NC

Figure 1 - J. Van Lindley Ancestors

John Isaac Lindley, 5th Great-Grandfather

The Oldest Recorded Ancestor

The oldest recorded ancestor for J. Van Lindley was his 5th Great Grandfather (7 generations prior) born on July 21, 1615 in Lindenlea, Cheshire, England. His name was John Isaac Lindley. He was married to Alice Crossharre, a woman 5 years younger, in 1638 in England. They had 2 children - Thomas, born in 1640, and James William, born in 1641 (T. M. Lindley).

According to some family genealogical records, John Isaac was imprisoned in England for his Quaker religious beliefs (T. M. Lindley). Attempts to confirm this independently with other records did not turn up a second source, but did confirm that there was widespread, and well documented, suffering by the Quakers during the mid-late 1600's. However, this particular family belief can be dismissed because at the time of John Isaac's death in 1641 the founder of the Quakers, George Fox, was only 17 years old. The Quaker religion was established by George Fox a few years later when George began preaching publicly in 1647 (Wikipedia).

John Isaac's unfortunate death left his spouse Alice a widow and raising two children alone at the tender of twenty-one. There are no known records about her fate or that of her older son Thomas following John Isaac's death, but there are records concerning her younger son James William Lindley, Senior.

The England to Ireland Quaker Movement

The first Irish Quaker meeting took place in 1654 (Mulcahy) and the first well-known Quaker missionaries came in 1655. Edward Burrough, 20 years of age, and Francis Howgil, 27, visited Dublin for 3 months, then split up, going to Kilkenny, Waterford, Younghall, and finally reuniting in Cork. There they were expelled from the nation by order of Henry Cromwell, Lord Deputy of Ireland (Backhouse, Backhouse and Mounsey). The success of these missionaries is doubtful, but the fact of their expulsion illustrates that the Quakers in the 1650s were considered a radical group and were perceived as a threat to the government.

The early Irish Quakers were generally young when they arrived from England. James William Lindley, Sr. at 30 years of age fits into this trend. Each one of them was a recent convert to the new religion. As a result of their youth and recent conversion, many of these individuals exhibited strong religious fervor. At that time in England, all Englishmen were required to pay tithes to the (Anglican) parish priests. The Quakers opposed paying tithes to a religious body that they did not believe in. This became one of the primary tenants of their faith and the cause of most of their suffering. To escape persecution, English Quakers moved to Ireland where almost all of the Quakers were English born or their parents were English. No evidence exists that there were any native Irish converts among them. The majority of the Quakers who arrived in the middle of the 1600s came from the northern half of England. The early Quakers, like other recent English settlers, looked down upon the native Irish.

Many of the most radical Quaker figures were dead by 1670, leading to a more conservative leadership. In Ireland, William Edmundson (a former Cromwellian soldier who converted) and George Fox introduced a hierarchical meeting structure to control and administer the "Society of Friends" (another name by which the Quakers became and are still known). A standard set of guidelines was introduced to regulate the conduct of members. "Plainness in speech, behavior and appeal" was a phrase which came to be used as the standard by which Quakers were judged. The Quakers came under the influence of Quietism. Quietism was a form of religious mysticism, which originated in Spain in the late 17th century. It required the withdrawal of the spirit from all human effort and complete passivity to God's will (Town of Mountmellick). Quakers initially attended and disrupted both Church of Ireland and Roman Catholic services in the 1660's and 1670's. There were 30 Quaker meetings (the name for their small, organized congregations) in Ireland by 1660 and 53 by 1701. In 1680 there were 798 Quaker families in Ireland, including that of James William and his wife Alice, and a total Quaker population estimated at about 6,000 members (Kilroy).

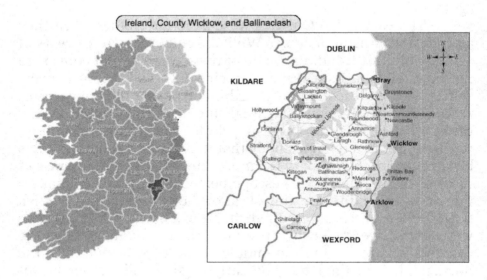

Figure 2 - County Wicklow and Ballinaclash, Ireland

James William Lindley, Senior, 4th Great-Grandfather

James William Lindley, Senior moved to Ireland some-time prior to his marriage there in 1677 at the age of 36. James married Alice Walsmith that year in Cronagallagh, County Wicklow, Ireland (Vann and Eversley). We can confirm that both John and Alice were Quakers. As a result of the Quaker desire to maintain a complete record of their sufferings, and as a disciplined faith, they kept meticulous records. They paid careful attention to maintaining accurate records of births, marriages, deaths, and membership. They even recorded applications for marriage, which included the occupation of both parties. "Testimonies" of how they came to faith were also written on the death of many Friends as part of their records (Tottenham Quakers). The marriage of James and Alice was included as part of the records of the Irish Wicklow Monthly Meeting (MM).

How and when James William Lindley got to Ireland is not exactly known. One unnamed source suggested that it was around 1670, when James was about 30 years old. We do know that he was there by 1677, when he was married at the age of 36. As an English-born Quaker living in Ireland, he was the original pioneer in what would become a family trait - moving to enjoy religious freedom and/or taking advantage of economic opportunities. His simple movement across the Irish Sea would become a precursor for many subsequent moves by his descendants. The vast majority of these descendants would also remain faithful Quakers for over 6 generations spread across 250 years. The faith and character of this boy who never knew his father must have been strong because his descendants followed his example into the early 20th century.

Alice and James William produced four children: Martha, James II, Thomas, and Mary. Four years after Mary's birth, when Martha was 13 years old, Alice died during the winter on February 16, 1691, leaving James William as a widower with four young children to rear. Understandably, just over two years later, he married Elizabeth Manliffe on April 26, 1693 in Wicklow. They had one child together, Isabella, in 1693. James William lived until he was 73 years old, dying on May 16, 1714 in Timullen, County Wicklow, Ireland. He was buried in Ballinaclash, Bally Moren, County Wicklow, Ireland.

A couple of years prior to James' death, both of his sons left Ireland for the British Colonies in America. James and Alice had produced some fervent Quakers. Their sons would each position themselves at the center of two important Quaker Colonial cities - Chester and Philadelphia - in the Quaker led colony of Pennsylvania. Our journey will follow James William Lindley, Junior and his descendants.

James William Lindley, Junior, 3ʳᵈ Great-Grandfather

Birth and Early Life

James William Lindley, Junior was born on April 16, 1681, five generations before J. Van Lindley, in the town of Ballinaclash, County Wicklow, Ireland. He married Eleanor Parke just short of his 24th birthday on April 14, 1705 in Kilconner Meeting, County Carlow, as recorded by the Wicklow Monthly Meeting, County Wicklow, Ireland (Historical Society of Pennsylvania). The couple had five children in Ireland prior to their migration to Pennsylvania. This family of seven was the first generation of Lindley ancestors of J. Van Lindley to come to America. They were received on certificate at the New Garden Monthly Meeting in Pennsylvania on August 3, 1713 (Myers). James purchased 200 acres of land in the same year (Futhey and Cope).

While there is not much documentation regarding James during his life in Ireland, there are some facts about Eleanor. Eleanor was the eldest daughter of five children born to Robert and Margery Parke. Eleanor had an uncle named Thomas Parke. Uncle Thomas owned several parcels of land in 1720 in three different places in Ireland - Ballilean, Ballaghmore, and Coolisnacktah. He sold his cattle and these three properties in 1724 and, along with seven of his ten children, crossed the Atlantic and arrived in Pennsylvania on August 21, 1724. The journey in those days typically took three months. Like Eleanor's family, her uncle and his family were aboard the ship for the entire summer. After arriving, they briefly stayed with other families, and then Uncle Thomas bought 500 acres from Thomas Lindley on December 1, 1724 (Futhey and Cope).

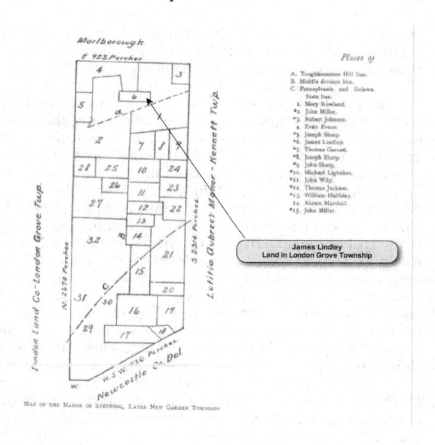

Figure 3 - James Lindley land in London Grove Township

Domestic Life and Land Purchases

New Garden Township in Chester County, Pennsylvania, where James and Eleanor settled, was land that had been granted to William Penn, Jr. as settlement of a debt owed to his father by the King of England. The debt repayment was for funds furnished by the elder Penn to help the King finance a war. Penn was given huge tracts of land, including a tract of 16,500 acres in Chester County (Futhey and Cope), of which Irish Quakers bought 5,413 acres at the rate of 20 pence per hundred (mrbuldog@sirius.com). Penn himself visited, but never lived in America and sold the land through agents. A second account of the cost of the land states that William Penn offered his lands for forty shillings (two pounds) per hundred acres, so the Irish Quakers appear to have received a greatly discounted price.

The economics of James' purchase at the time are astounding. Understanding the economic incentive helps to understand why James and his family left Ireland and risked the transatlantic voyage. If we assume that James bought his land at 20 pence per hundred and that he bought at least 1000 acres, he would have paid 200 pence. At the time, a pound was divided into 20 shillings and each shilling into 12 pence. This means that 240 pence equaled a pound at that time. By this measure, James paid less than 1 pound for 1000 acres. Using the second account of the cost of the land of two pounds per hundred acres, James would have paid twenty pounds for 1000 acres. Given this range, we can conclude that James paid between one and twenty pounds for 1000 acres of fresh, heavily timbered land. By comparison, at the same time, land in England sold for 20 to 60 pounds for one acre. In addition, annual rent on the land in England was one to three pounds per acre while James paid one shilling per acre.

Several records remain, which help give clues as to James Lindley Jr.'s life and status. In a book about early Irish Quaker immigration, of the twenty-two persons taxed in New Garden in 1715, fifteen were Irish Friends, listed in descending order as follows:

Mary Miller, 9s. (9 shillings)
James Lindley, 4s. 6d. (4 shillings, 6 pence)
Thomas Garnett, 3s. 9d.
John Sharp, 3s. 6d.
Thomas Jackson, 3s.
James Starr, 3s.
William Halliday, 2s. 7d.
John Wiley, 2s. 4d.
Benjamin Fred, 2s. 1d
Joseph Sharp, 2s.
Margaret Lowden, 2s.
Michael Lightfoot, 2s.

Francis Hobson, 2s.
Joseph Garnett, 2s.
Robert Johnson, 2s.

In 1722, James Lindley purchased an additional 400 acres in the adjoining town of London Grove and in the next year became the first constable of the Township of London Grove. Of the 43 taxable persons in this township in 1722, James Lindley's tax of 19 shillings was the largest.

A few years later, in 1724, out of forty-two taxable persons in London Grove there were ten Irish Friends:

James Lindley, 19s.
Michael Harlan, Sr., 13s. 4d.
Joseph Sharp, 13s.
John Allen, 8s.
John Cane, 7s.
Jeremiah Starr, 4s. 6d.
Robert Cane, 4s.
Moses Harlan, 4s.
Michael Harlan, Jr., 2s. 4d.
Joseph Garnett, 1s. 8d.

James subsequently purchased another 600 acres in 1726 and was described in legal documents as either a blacksmith or a yeoman (a person who owns or cultivates a small farm). He was one of the largest landowners in the Toughkenemon Valley, an area southeast of Philadelphia today still known as New Garden Township in Chester County, with a recorded estate of at least 600 acres. One of Uncle Thomas Parke's children wrote a letter to his sister Mary Parke Valentine in England in October of 1725. He was eager to convince his sister and her family to join them. Most of his letter tries to dispel unfounded rumors regarding the colony. Then cousin Thomas also passes on some news:

"Unkle James Lindley and family is well and
thrives exceedingly, he has 11 children and reaped

last harvest about 800 bushels of wheat, he is a
thriving man anywhere he lives, he has a thousand
acres of land, a fine estate."

Since James had purchased the raw, undeveloped land
about 10 years before the arrival of these relatives, this account
reflects that he had been busy developing the land by clearing,
planting, and growing crops. His development of the land led to
crop production, the 800 bushels of wheat that Robert Parke
refers to in his letter. (As a comparison, in the early 1900's, the
average yield per acre was 12-14 bushels. Assuming slightly
more primitive methods, at 8-10 bushels per acre, James would
have been working 80-100 acres dedicated solely to the production of wheat.) James, the first Lindley in America, set a high
standard for work effort. He worked the land using horses or
mules and primitive plows, kept a blacksmith business going,
and cleared additional acreage. He most likely had his family
working beside him every step of the way because there was
little hired labor at the time except indentured servants, but
there is no indication that he had much help outside his family,
apart from the "one servant man" mentioned in his will (Myers).

James' Death, Inventory and Will

James died in 1726, only 13 years after arriving in Colonial Pennsylvania. He was 45 years old when he died on October
13, 1726. James's eleven-year-old son, William, died just 13 days
later. It is possible that a disease or sickness had struck the
family. Eleanor subsequently gave birth to their twelfth child
just three months after James death. For the second time in 3
generations, one of J. Van Lindley's direct ancestors left a widow
with small children. Eleanor was 43 at her husband's death with
two children over 18, but another ten under 18. Eleanor married
once again in 1730 to a man named Henry Jones.

As a man of means, James Lindley Jr. died with an inventory of his property and a will that was recorded and kept with
West Chester Pennsylvania historical records, as evidenced by
the following account:

"It is the inventory of James Lindley, smith, of London Grove, Chester County, who had the most considerable estate of any of those mentioned:

Purs and apparell £22. 12s
7 Beds and Furniture thereto belonging
1 Chest of Drawers
2 Chests
2 Boxes
And 1 Looking glass;
4 Table Cloaths
13 Sheets and 1 Warming pan;
2 Pieces of Stuff and
1 Sett of New Curtains;
Fflax,
1 hackle,
Chains,
Salt box,
Iron pots & Candle sticks;
2 mens Saddles
2 weomans Sadles
1 Pillion &
2 Bridles;
Wool Cards,
Sole Leather,
Pewter,
Brass Tin, &
wooden ware;
to Baggs,
Mault,
Indian Corn,
Salt,
Wheels, &
a half Bushell;
Irons in the Kitchen,
Coopers ware &
Earthen ware &c;
Dressed Skin,
Books

Iron,
Steel
2 whip saws &
1 Cross;
Carpenters Tools,
Pincers,
Hows,
Plows,
Harrows &
Ox Chains;
Grinding Stones,
Coles,
Bells,
Shovells, and
forks &c;
A Cart with the Geers and Chains,
hooks,
hors Shoes;
Oak Boards,
Scantling,
3 Guns & Bullet Moulds;
Grubing Axes,
Well Chain,
Wolf Trap,
falling axes &c;
Sickles,
Sythes and
Doe Trough;
Corn in the Barn, and
Corn in the Mill;
Corn in the Ground,
Hay in the Meadow;
16 horses, Mares and Colts;
27 Cows, Oxen and Young Cattle;
10 Sheep and Swine;
Smiths Tools in the Shop;
one Servant Man;
5 Bonds and one Bill;

Book Debts;
Plantation and Improvements"
[Total value £1115.9s.8d.]

A researcher made the following note after listing this inventory:

> "The bells mentioned, no doubt, were those attached to cattle and sheep in order to trace the animals in their wanderings through the woods. This is the only reference to a 'Looking glass' that I have noted in the inventories" (Myers).

The Will for James Lindley goes into more detail in explaining how his estate is divided:

Name: James Lindley
Title: Smith
Description: Decedent
Residence: Londongrove
Date: 8 Oct 1726
Prove Date: 2 Jan 1726
Book Page: A: 210

James Lindley of Londongrove. Smith. 10/8/1726. January 2, 1726/7. A. 210.

To wife 200 acres of land being 1/2 of the tract I now live on and all personal estate. She to pay for the 600 acres I have got an order to have surveyed of the land of Sir John Faggs.

To sons Thomas, James, Robert and William 200 acres of land each when 21, that is the above 600 acres divided into 3 equal parts and the remaining half of the tract I now live on, to son Jonathan the plantation I now live on at death of wife, to daughter Rachel £20 at 21, to daughter Margarey, £20 at 21, to daughter Elizabeth £20 at 21, to daughter

Hannah £20 at 21, [also provides for a child yet to be born] to son James the smith tools.

Executors: wife Elinor and son Thomas.

Witnesses: Susanna Wilcocks, Elish Maxwell, John Jordan (Chester County).

The will may well have reflected the customs of the day. Each son received an equal portion of land at maturity, defined as age 21. Each daughter received an equal payment in currency at maturity. Was this equitable? The daughters were paid 20 pounds sterling, which equals the higher end of what James had paid during the previous 13 years for his 1000 acres of land. His estate was valued at £1115.9s.8d in total. If his total land ownership was 1000 acres - 400 acres that he lived on, plus the 600 acres that Sir John Faggs was surveying, and most of his wealth was in his land, we could estimate that his land was worth approximately one-pound sterling per acre at death. A comparison of the 20 pounds sterling inheritance of the daughters with the land holding inheritance of 200 acres per boy leads to the conclusion that the land the boys received was probably worth ten times what the girls received.

There is one curiosity concerning the will. Two daughters, Alice and Mary, born in 1716 and 1717, are not mentioned in the will. They were older than Elizabeth, Hannah, Jonathan, and an unborn child - all of which were provided for in the will. Had they died already? Given that, if alive, they would have been 9 and 10 years old in 1726, most likely they were already dead at the time of James' death.

The funeral expenses for James Lindley, of London Grove, as shown by the accounts filed by his executors, were £4. 10s. and "ye Coffin" £1. 8s (Myers).

Life Summary

James took a big risk, bringing his family as some of the first settlers in a wild and untamed land. But, the risk paid off with a handsome reward, directly due to James' personal work effort. While working as a blacksmith he was also able to clear land, plant seed, and grow wheat. There is no indication of how much wealth he possessed upon entering the Colony of Pennsylvania, yet by the time of his death he was known as the wealthiest person in his area. James was one of the earliest pioneers and therefore one of the earliest examples of someone who lived the "The American Dream." Over 50 years before the American Revolution, he was able to have the opportunity to quickly achieve significant wealth by taking risks and working hard. He left his children with a share of the wealth he created, but more importantly he was a role model for his descendants by demonstrating how to succeed in America.

The oldest son of James, Thomas Lindley, turned 21 the same year his father died. Thomas had already been working beside his father in this new world for 13 years by the time of his father's death. He had helped clear the land and create the new wealth. At the young age of 21 he was about to take on even more responsibility.

Thomas Lindley, Senior, 2nd Great-Grandfather

Birth to Age 21

James Lindley's oldest son was named Thomas Lindley and was later known as Thomas Lindley, Senior. Thomas was J. Van Lindley's 2nd Great Grandfather. He was born in 1706 in Ballinaclash, Ireland. Thomas was seven years old when his family moved to the Colony of Pennsylvania in 1713. The family consisted of five children and two parents when they moved. Since James was a blacksmith (also known as an ironmonger) and a farmer, Thomas probably spent time helping his father from the time they landed in the new world. The land his father bought from William Penn had to be cleared, planted and maintained.

When his father died thirteen years later at the age of 41 in 1726, Thomas was only a few months shy of his 21st birthday. By that time, eleven children had been born to his parents and a twelfth was on the way. According to the terms of his father's will, 600 acres, which had been surveyed, bought and paid for, was divided between Thomas and two of his brothers. Thomas therefore inherited 200 acres of land when he turned 21 on February 25, 1727. Based upon the previously mentioned calculations at the time of his father's death, the value of the land was probably worth about 200 pounds sterling.

The reality of Thomas's life at the young age of 20 and 21 was that, as the oldest of 12 children with probably 9 living, he became the "man of the house." As the oldest son, he had already been intimately involved with and experienced at both blacksmithing and farming. His responsibilities most likely involved keeping the entire family operation going. His brother James was probably involved as well, being just 3 years younger. Until his mother remarried, the two of them would have had the primary responsibility for operating the farm. The widow Eleanor married Henry Jones in 1730 and this event gave the two older boys a chance to begin to work their own land. Thomas might have been eager to step out on his own by this time.

Thomas Lindley Marries Ruth Hadley

On October 21, 1731 Thomas married Ruth Hadley. Ruth was the daughter of Simon Hadley, Jr. Like Thomas's father James William Lindley, Jr., Simon was well off and a prominent Quaker landowner.

Unfortunately, the next year Thomas's younger brother James died. Four sons had been given 200 acres each in the will - Thomas, James, Robert and William. William died in 1726, just after his father, and now James in 1732. That left only two sons - Thomas and Robert. Robert was mentioned as being disowned by the New Garden Quaker Monthly Meeting when he was 20 in 1732. Beyond that entry, no further documentation of his marriage, death or other event could be found. It is possible that Thomas eventually inherited all of his father's estate.

Thomas and Ruth Hadley have children

Thomas and Ruth raised their family in the Colony of Pennsylvania until 1753. They had eight children born in London Grove, Chester County, Pennsylvania. Three of the eight were girls and five were boys. J. Van Lindley's Great Grandfather was the fourth child and was named Thomas Lindley, Jr. He was born in 1740 and was 13 years old when his father decided to move to North Carolina (Hinshaw).

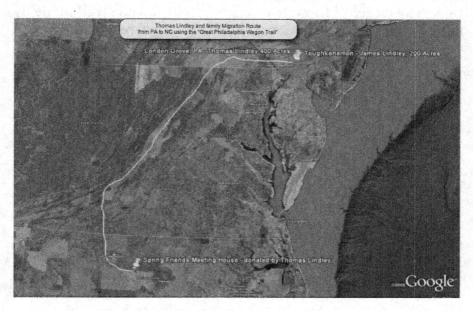

Figure 4 - Pennsylvania to North Carolina Migration Route

Thomas Lindley, Sr. Moves and Buys Land

In 1753, at the age of 47, Thomas, Sr.:

"...requested a certificate for himself, wife and children to Cane Creek M.M., North Carolina." One month later, April 26, 1753, the certificate was approved but Thomas did not present it to Cane Creek Meeting until October 6, 1753, more than

five months later. The Cane Creek records indicate
that Deborah and a younger brother, Jonathan,
were born in Orange County (now Alamance),
North Carolina, and that the eight older children
were born in Pennsylvania" (H. Newlin).

The family migrated to North Carolina. There were no roads,
just paths at the time. Travel from Pennsylvania to North Carolina could have followed two routes - both following Indian
trails. The larger of these two was originally a wide trail made by
buffalo migrations that became known as the Great Philadelphia
Wagon Trail and was the one taken by Thomas Lindley:

"In the eighteenth century, few migrations trails in
America were more important than the Indian
route, which extended east of the Appalachians
from Pennsylvania to Georgia. This Ancient Warriors Path had long been used by the Iroquois
tribesmen of the north to come to the south and
trade or to make war in Virginia and the Carolinas.
By a series of treaties with the powerful Five Na-
tions of the Iroquois, the English acquired the use
of the Warriors Path. After 1744 they took over the
land itself. The growth of the route into the princi-
pal highway of the colonial backcountry was important in the development of the nation. Over this
vast wagon road came the English, Scots-Irish and
German settlers to claim land. The Great Warriors
Path led from the Iroquois Confederacy around the
Great Lakes through what later became the Pennsylvania towns of Lancaster, Bethlehem, York, and
Gettysburg, into western Maryland around what is
now known as Hagerstown, across the Potomac
River at Evan Watkins Ferry following the narrow
path across the 'back country' or 'up country' or
'Piedmont' to Winchester through the Shenandoah
Valley of Virginia to Harrisonburg, Staunton, Lex-
ington, and Roanoke before heading into the

North Carolina towns of Salem and Salisbury,
where the route joined the east–west Catawba and
Cherokee Indian Trading Path at the Trading Ford
across the Yadkin River, in Rowan, North Carolina..." (McPherson Compton)

After traveling down the Great Philadelphia Wagon Trail,
Thomas then took the Cherokee Indian Trading Path east (today
Interstate 85 in North Carolina runs east-west along almost the
exact same path). He found the land he wanted to buy just south
of the Trading Path - land along Cane (also known as "Cain")
Creek. Cane Creek is a tributary of the Haw River. The Haw
River flows southeast from central North Carolina, becoming
the Cape Fear River before it empties into the Atlantic Ocean.
Thomas chose the location along Cane Creek because it was near
a newly formed Quaker Monthly Meeting named Cane Creek
Monthly Meeting. The water of Cane Creek ran through the
center of Thomas's land and provided easy access for irrigation
of his farm. Interesting in terms of today's geography, the land
he bought was considered in the "far west" of North Carolina at
that time. The land had been owned by the Earl of Granville and
was part of a large piece of land known as "The Granville District" which was:

"...a 60-mile wide strip of land in the North Carolina colony adjoining the boundary with Virginia,
lying between north latitudes 35° 34' and 36° 30'"
(Hofmann).

Why did Thomas leave Pennsylvania? Once again, it can
be attributed to economic opportunity. A fifty-acre farm in
Lancaster County, PA cost 7 pounds 10 shillings by 1750. In the
Granville District of North Carolina, five shillings would buy 100
acres (Hofmann).

The Cane Creek Valley

The area where Thomas Lindley settled was along the Cane Creek. Cane Creek is located in southeastern Alamance County in North Carolina. At the time that Thomas Lindley first saw the land it was part of the newly created Orange County, an area which later became part of Chatham County and today is part of Alamance County. The Cane Creek Mountains rise up to a height of just over 900 feet, cresting with the Cane Creek Mountain at 987 feet. Bass Mountain is also part of this chain that forms the northern boundary of land that drains into Cane Creek. Cane Creek itself flows from west to east over a 10-12 mile area, also collecting water from more gradual southern and western elevations that only rise to 625-650 feet. The creek meanders back and forth at a level of about 450 feet until it finally empties into the Haw River 3 miles north of the southeast corner of Alamance County, where it borders northern Chatham County.

The term "mountains," when used to describe land that rises just 500 feet above their surroundings, is somewhat of a misnomer, but they were an important geological feature since they collected and channeled the water used by colonial farmers to grow their crops. Thomas Lindley chose his land with the intention of farming the land. Over 250 years later, land in the same area is still farmed by some of his descendants, so his choice of farmland has been thoroughly justified (Wikipedia).

The Granville District

The Granville District, which includes the Cane Creek area, was originally a part of the Province of Carolina. This province was a "proprietary colony" under the control of eight Lord Proprietors from 1663 to 1729. In 1729, seven of the eight heirs to the original Lords Proprietor decided to sell their shares back to the crown.

The eighth share belonged to John Carteret, 2nd Earl of Granville, and the great-grandson of the original Lord Proprietor, Sir George Carteret. Unlike the other heirs, he surrendered any participation in government in order to retain ownership in his one-eighth share of the colony's land.

Due to political reversals in England, John Carteret was unable to attend to his colonial interests until 1742. The king's Privy Council agreed to Carteret's request to plan his allotment. He began by appointing the first of several agents who operated on his authority in the district. He was never able to visit the colony in person. The task was given to Samuel Warner, a London surveyor, who determined that Carteret was entitled to fifty-six and a quarter minutes of north latitude. This northern boundary became the Virginia-North Carolina border (36° 30') and the southern boundary line for his land was placed at 35° 34'. In 1743, a commission appointed jointly by Carteret and the North Carolina Governor Gabriel Johnston surveyed the initial portion of the boundary line. The line was extended westward in 1746 and again in 1753. In 1744, Carteret inherited the title Earl of Granville, and from that time, the district became known as Granville's district or the Granville district (Wikipedia).

The 1753 extension of Granville's tract added a large county named Orange, which included the land where Thomas Lindley decided to settle. Although there were already some settlers in that area, when the land became classified as a county, it also canonized the process for attaining legally recognized ownership. Thomas Lindley, Sr. initially purchased two pieces of land in Orange County. The process for buying land from Granville involved a multi-step process:

> First, the settler had to identify the land, stake it out, and tell the land official where and how much land was desired.

> Second, they had to get a land warrant from the land official with instructions to the official surveyor to complete a survey within 6 months.

> Third, they surveyor would go to the land, find the tract, survey it, and make several copies of the survey.

Finally, the settler had one year from the date of
the survey's completion to pay the required fees
and receive an indenture. Failure to complete the
process within the allotted time led to the warrant
expiring. If this happened, the land would again
become available for a new settler (Dobbs)
(Hofmann).

Land Purchases

Thomas attempted to buy several pieces of land, utilizing
the newly established process:

The first tract was identified as "No. 85" and was
for 356 acres. On the survey, a notation is made
that it was entered on April 26, 1753 along with the
words: "This Plan represents a tract of Land Surveyed for Alex Mebane lying on the South Side of
Cain Creek and the North side of Haw River above
the Piney Mountain." The survey was made on
February 26, 1755 and the Deed was issued November 13, 1756 in Orange County (NC, Office of
Secretary of State).

Figure 5 - Survey of 356 acres bought by Thomas Lindley, Sr.

The second piece of land was identified as "No. 21" and was for a 640 acre tract "on the South East side of Cain Creek, on the East side of Haw River, on the Tract that goes out of Mitchell's Path to John Gray." The land warrant was dated February 26, 1755. No survey or indenture was found in the N.C. State Archives for this tract (NC, Office of Secretary of State).

The third piece of land was identified as "No. 18" and was a 600-acre tract "on the South prong of Cain Creek, at a place called Fisher's Place, formerly surveyed by Zacariah Martinson." This tract was laid out in a rectangle. It measured 60 chains across, running East-West, and 100 chains down, running North-South. One square chain equals 1/10 of an acre, so the 60 x 100 chain measurement equaled 6000 square chains or 600 acres. Across the middle, running from lower left, 20% up from the southern border, to almost upper right, 95% across from the western border ran the South Fork of Cane Creek, bisecting the property and providing central water access for easy irrigation. The land warrant was dated February 3, 1756 for this property. William Churton, the official surveyor, surveyed the land on May 8, 1756. The indenture for this acreage was not processed until February 22, 1759 and had an identification of "No. 66" and another with the "No. 66" crossed out and "No. 1476" written instead [by that time, the original warrant should have expired worthless], but was recorded as "Orange 1756" (NC, Office of Secretary of State Granville Proprietary Land Office).

The fourth tract was identified as "No. 49" and was 200 acres in Cumberland County on the "upper side of the Lower Little River." This property survey order was entered on September 22, 1766. This land would not have been contiguous with the other land holdings, but may have been bought in anticipation of building another gristmill. No survey or indenture was found in the N.C. State Archives for this tract (NC, Office of Secretary of State).

It appears that Thomas successfully bought tracts for 600 and 356 acres from Lord Granville in Orange/Chatham County for a total of 956 acres between 1753 and 1756. Thomas's indenture included an agreement to pay 3 shillings per 100 acres annually in exchange for the deed to the land. In addition, he may have purchased another 600 acres in Orange/Chatham and 200 acres in Cumberland County, but the records are not complete, which probably means that they were surveyed, but never purchased.

The Deed Process in Orange County

From the earliest days of North Carolina until the close of the year 1863 deeds were approved or acknowledged before judges in the County Court during their quarterly sessions. Probate, or proof, of a deed was performed by one of the witnesses to the deed appearing in a court and swearing that his signature on the instrument was in fact his signature, and that the instrument was the deed it purported to be. When probate was by acknowledgment, the grantor appeared in person at the court with the instrument and acknowledged to the judges that he had made the conveyance to the grantee.

When the judge accepted the proof or had knowledge of the genuineness of the deed, he then ordered the deed to be recorded. The clerk of the court sent the deed to the register of deeds. The register of deeds copied the deed into a deed book (after the grantee paid the registration fee) and returned the original deed to the grantee. Registers' deed books were protected by law and passed on from each county register to their successor. Their job was to protect the real property titles and insure that the records were respected and preserved.

Unfortunately, Orange County's colonial deed books fell into the hands of a man with a grudge and he neither respected nor preserved the books. When the town of Hillsboro fell into the hands of the British Army in 1781, the British Tory, James Munro, seized the deed books. Munro's property and private business papers had been confiscated, and he intended to hold the deed books as ransom. In order to hide them from the Americans, Munro buried the Orange County deed books in a wooded area near the town and went on his way, leaving them to rot in the ground.

Munro's act of retaliation left a gap in the Orange County deed books from 1752 through 1781. One early book containing deeds proved from the June court of 1755 through June of 1756 escaped Munro's clutches and is now Book One. Book Two contains the few deeds from 1752 through 1781 that were recorded, as well as the deeds proved from 1782 until part way through 1785. Excluding these noted exceptions, the gap in the records is an empty void.

To try to reconstruct the records, the probate of deeds recorded in the court minutes were extracted by the clerk of court into a separate volume during the years from 1752 through 1768. This helped to fill half of the period for which there are no surviving deed books. (Into the same volume later a clerk noted each deed proved during the year 1793.) This volume is now located in the North Carolina archives.

The devastating result is a nearly 30-year gap in the records with no surviving description for most land transactions. There are individual clues and confirmations in the names of grantors, grantees, witnesses, acknowledgments, acreage, and probate dates in the court records, but in general the records are either fragmentary or do not exist.

The impact of this event is that it is not now possible to determine the amount of acreage owned by Thomas Lindley, Sr. or the exact location of his properties. Based upon the court records of Orange County, N.C., there are records of four land purchases by Thomas Lindley, Senior:

> The first was on December 11, 1753 when he was 47 years old. There is a deed of sale from "Hugh Lauglen" to an unknown person because of a tear in the deed. However, in October of 1754 William Churton testified in court that there was a deed of sale to Thomas Lindley for 305 acres of land. Even in this case, the handwriting is not clear and it could be 303 acres of land, but the court registered the deed. No location is given for where this land is located.

The second purchase was in July of 1754 from Zachariah Martin, Senior for 640 acres. It also had to be proved in court by an oath by Zachariah Martin, Junior, which was enough to register the deed. Unfortunately, there was again no location given.

The third and fourth purchases were grants of land from Lord Granville for 356 and 600 acres. The former was Grant #85, completed on May 11, 1757. The latter was originally Grant #66, which was changed to #147, and was completed on February 2, 1759. The location of both grants was described as being: "On the south fork of Cane Creek and west side of the Haw River." Both property descriptions start on Cane creek and proceed south, putting the properties on the south side of the creek.

These four purchases totaled 1901 acres.

There are also records of three sales:

> *The first is the sale of 200 acres recorded to "Francis Jones, saddler" on January 14, 1755.*

> *The second is the sale to "John Spurlin" on May 12, 1761, but the amount of acreage is left blank.*

> *The third is the sale of 300 acres to his son, Thomas Lindley, Junior on August 13, 1765 (Bennett) (E. B. Weeks).*

The Grist Mill

The early Orange County records in Hillsboro, North Carolina contain the following agreement:

"Hugh Laughlin, Planter, on the one part, and Thomas Lindley, Planter, on the other, have

agreed to become partners and in joint company to
erect and build a water grist mill on Cane Creek,
on the south side of Haw River. The water to be
taken out of the part of land owned by Hugh
Laughlin and the mill to be built on that part
owned by Thomas Lindley three and three quar-
ters acres.

September Court, 1755" (Bennett).

The millpond and race were on Hugh McLaughlin's land and the
mill was placed just across the line on Thomas Lindley's land, as
noted in the agreement. The gristmill became the first gristmill
in the valley and can be found as a landmark on many early
maps of the area. The gristmill has been in operation since the
two partners started and continues today under the sole ownership of the Lindley family.

Simon Hadley Jr. dies

Simon Hadley Jr., Ruth Hadley Lindley's father, died in
1756 with a will that has been preserved. In the will, regarding
his daughter Ruth, he said:

"I do leave my daughter, Ruth Lindley, wife of
Thomas Lindley, ten pounds current money and I
do leave to the said Thomas Lindley, ten pounds
current money, which shall be in full their portion
and share of my real and personal estate" (1756
Will of Simon Hadley).

In addition, Simon provided even more generously for his
9 grandchildren:

"I do leave to my grandchildren, to Catherine
Lindley, sixty pounds current money, and I do
leave James Lindley sixty pounds current money
and I do leave Simon Lindley sixty pounds current
money and I do leave Ruth Lindley, Jr. sixty

pounds current money, and I do leave Mary Lindley, Jr. sixty pounds current money, and I do leave Ellenor Lindley sixty pounds current money and I do leave William Lindley sixty pounds current money and I do leave Thomas Lindley, Jr. sixty pounds current money, all children of my daughter Ruth Lindley, wife to Thomas Lindley and I do leave Deborah Lindley sixty pounds current money" (1756 Will of Simon Hadley).

Simon included all his grandchildren except two - John and Jonathan. Jonathan was born the same year, so his exclusion is understandable, but John, a 9 year-old, who lived until 1790, may have been an oversight.

The Regulator Movement

Beginning about 1750, the Earl of Granville became concerned about irregularities in the accounts from his agents in the issuance of land grants, so he issued explicit instructions about keeping records and executing grants. Despite Granville's specific instructions to his agents, complaints from land holders and prospective purchasers increased throughout the 1750s; particularly allegations of exorbitant fees.

After the Earl's death in 1763, the situation became more muddled when settlers were unable to obtain clear title to the land they were purchasing. This led to outbreaks of violence in 1770 in what were then the western regions (centered in present-day Alamance County), which were put down by Governor William Tryon.

In 1764, several thousand people from North Carolina, mainly from Orange, Anson, and Granville counties in the western region, were extremely dissatisfied with the wealthy North Carolina officials whom they considered cruel, arbitrary, tyrannical and corrupt. Local sheriffs supported by the courts collected taxes; the sheriffs and courts had sole control over their local regions. Many of the officers were deemed to be very greedy and often would band together with other local officials for their own personal gain. The entire system depended on the integrity of local officials, many of whom engaged in extortion; taxes collected often enriched the tax collectors directly. At times, sheriffs would intentionally remove records of their tax collection in order to further tax citizens. The colonial governor, who feared losing the support of the various county officials, endorsed the system. It was a struggle between mostly lower class citizens, who made up the majority of the population of North Carolina, and the wealthy ruling class, who comprised about 5% of the population, yet maintained almost total control of the government.

The primary aim of the Regulators was to form an honest government and reduce taxation. The wealthy business-men/politicians that ruled North Carolina saw this as a grave threat to their power. Ultimately, they brought in the militia to crush the rebellion, and then hanged the leaders. It is estimated that out of the 8,000 people living in Orange County at the time, some six or seven thousand of them were in support of the Regulators. Although the "War of the Regulators" is considered by some to be one of the first acts of the American Revolutionary War, it was waged against corrupt local officials and not against the king or crown. In reality, many anti-Regulators went on to become Whigs (Patriots) during the American Revolution and many other Regulators became Tories (Loyalists) (Lefler and Wager).

Thomas Lindley was politically involved in the Regulator movement (Lefler and Wager). In 1768 he was moved by the evidence of a miscarriage of justice to identify himself with the Regulator movement, which shook the communities across the piedmont sections of North and South Carolina and which in 1771 exploded in the War of the Regulators. During the early period of the movement he was looked to as one of the local leaders. In 1768 he was evidently a member of the Regulator committee appointed to wrestle with the problem of freeing the people of these interior counties from the abuse of their rights and the exploitation of their resources by officials of the colonial Government. A meeting of the Committee that was set to meet at the Lindley home on May 11, 1768 (Lefler and Wager) was not

held because of the arrest of some of the leaders of the movement. There is no documented evidence that Thomas Lindley
ever had any sympathy for the military action, which accompanied the Regulator Movement (A. I. Newlin, The Newlin Family
Ancestors and Descendants of John and Mary Pyle Newlin).

Thomas Lindley was directly impacted by the Regulator
conflict on Tuesday, May 21 when the royal government made a
requisition from the Quaker settlement at Cane Creek for six
wagonloads of flour for his majesty's service. The following day:

> "The Quakers on Cane Creek reporting that the
> flour required was stopped by the Regulators, the
> Governor ordered the detachment of Cumberland
> and Wake the Light Horse to march immediately
> to escort the flour to camp."

Finally, the third day:

> "The detachments of the preceding day arrived in
> camp from Lindley's and Dixon's Mills with nine
> loads of flour, making seventy barrels."

The incident did not end there because Governor Tryon
neglected to compensate the Quakers for the flour he had com-
mandeered. Apparently, he also confiscated the six wagons and
teams used to haul the flour. On November 7, 1772, at the
Monthly Meeting at Cane Creek, the Quakers addressed a
petition to the Governor (Tyron's successor, Josiah Martin), the
Council, the Speaker and members of the General Assembly.
Thomas and William Lindley were among the signers. After
consideration of this subject at their February, 1773 meeting, the
General Assembly disallowed the claim, which included 30
pounds due to Thomas Lindley out of a total 58-pound request.
The only surviving record says that the claim was "under con-
sideration," not indicating whether or not it was paid (S. B.
Weeks).

With the Johnston Riot of 1771, the Regulator movement
basically came to an end (Sheets). The existing Regulators that

were not involved in the leadership positions of the movement were given amnesty if they would swear allegiance under oath to support the crown (Saunders). Thomas was not listed as having done this for two reasons. One reason is that Quakers would only give their oath to God. The British governor Tryon made an allowance for this fact and the Quakers were given the choice of "affirming" allegiance. Thomas did not do an affirmation either, but instead chose silence (Sheets).

Granville's son, Robert Carteret, 3rd Earl Granville, became concerned by these problems and considered selling the land back to the crown, but this never happened and the situation continued to worsen with accurate records no longer being kept. When the younger Granville died in February 1776, revolutionary fervor was already strong and the proprietorship of the Granville district was identified with British interests. In 1777, the North Carolina assembly declared the new state as sovereign over all the lands between Virginia and South Carolina while recognizing claims to land granted by the crown and proprietors prior to July 4, 1776. The new State of North Carolina confiscated all lands and property of persons who supported the British during the war. Following the war, the Carteret heirs were compensated in part for the loss of their lands (Hofmann).

Spring Monthly Meeting

Thomas and Ruth Hadley Lindley and their nine children, along with Henry and Mary Faye Holladay and their three children, appear to have been the first Quakers to settle in the Spring Community. They were accompanied by a recently married couple, Hugh and Mary Evans Laughlin, who were not members of the Society of Friends. These three families selected adjoining tracts of land, all bordering on Cane Creek. Within a few years others followed these initial settlers, including Thomas's sister Mary Lindley Woody, her husband John, and two families that would intermarry with the Lindleys - the Braxtons and the Newlins.

Thomas and Ruth donated land for the first Spring Meeting house, property on which families still meet for Monthly Meetings 250 years later. The meetinghouse was started by 1761, was made into a Preparative Meeting in 1779, and a regular Monthly Meeting in 1793. Thomas and Ruth were buried in the cemetery, which today lies across the road today from the Spring Monthly Meeting building (A. I. Newlin, Friends "at the Spring:" a history of Spring Monthly Meeting).

Thomas Lindley's Children Choose Sides

The Revolutionary War, also known as the War for American Independence, began in June of 1775. Thomas was 69 years old by that date with grown children and teenage grandchildren. Historians have estimated that approximately 40-45% of the colonists actively supported the rebellion (known at the time as "Whigs" but predominately referred to within this book as "Patriots"), while 15-20% of the population of the thirteen colonies remained loyal to the British Crown (known as "Tories" or, as referred to in this book, "Loyalists"). The remaining 35-45% attempted to remain neutral (Calhoon). The Lindley children were split just like the rest of the country. James, the oldest son, was a Loyalist officer and was hanged on February 14, 1779 in the fort at Ninety-Six, South Carolina by the Patriots after his unit lost the Battle of Kettle Creek in nearby Wilkes County Georgia. John Lindley (along with his cousin William) was also an officer with Colonel John Pyle, MD, a noted Loyalist in Orange County. Meanwhile, Thomas' youngest son Jonathan was a supporter of the Patriots. The remaining children were not known to have an affiliation and may have been, as expected from a Quaker, neutral.

The Revolutionary War Battle of Lindley Mill

The Battle of Lindley Mill was a revolutionary battle fought entirely on the 956 acres of land owned by Thomas Lindley. The battle's storyline is full of intrigue, valiant fighting, and ambiguities about who really won. The one clear conclusion was that it was a hard fought battle, at close range, mostly between soldiers on both sides residing in North Carolina, with over 200 of the 1200 participants ending up dead or seriously wounded.

The story began with the famous British General Charles Cornwallis. A few months prior to his surrender to General George Washington, Cornwallis's British Army was trying to consolidate control over the interior areas of the Carolinas. As part of this campaign, he travelled through the Cane Creek area. His army marched just south and west of Thomas Lindley's land, in the vicinity of the Cane Creek Monthly Meeting. During the Revolution, the Cane Creek area was divided in its loyalties. Cornwallis found Loyalist sympathizers in the Cane Creek area. The creek represented a dividing line because north and east of the creek there was a hotbed of former Regulators who were strong Patriots (those desiring to break free from England's rule), while south of the creek could be found Loyalists (those whose interests remained behind continued English rule).

Cornwallis, en route to Hillsboro prior to the Battle of Guilford Courthouse, gathered recruits from the Cane Creek area, but they did not include the Quaker Thomas Lindley, who remained neutral. Cornwallis slept in a stone house in the area and sat in a chair while staying in Cane Creek. Thomas C. Dixon, a Loyalist sympathizer, kept the chair. The tradition held that Cornwallis, in an attempt to make sure that the Patriots might not capture him and his troops, had his cannon thrown into a local millpond or buried in the Cane Creek Cemetery. The tradition further stated that it was not subsequently removed and may remain there today (Barefoot, 1998).

Herman Husbands (a well known Regulator that had opposed the government) was also a Quaker. In the old meetinghouse at Cane Creek, he had married Mary Pugh. Herman was known to "speak his mind," and to be a leader, a man that others followed. Mary's brother Hugh also lived close by, was a Regulator and had killed 17 men when he lay behind a rock at the Battle of Alamance, so even within the Cane Creek congregation not all followers were Loyalists.

Thomas Lindley's land, where the Battle of Lindley Mill was fought, lay alongside Cane Creek five or six miles east of the Cane Creek Meeting House. The Battle of Lindley Mill was fought primarily on the north side of Cane Creek, with the initial battle line being primarily drawn along Stafford Branch, a small tributary that feeds from the northwest into the creek. The tributary is barely a yard wide, putting the two sides into close proximity, greatly increasing the casualties. Lindley Mill lies about 300 yards west of this battle line and was just beyond the battle area. However, it was the closest landmark and was used to identify the location of the conflict, so the Revolutionary War battle became known as "The Battle of Lindley Mill."

Cornwallis' troop movements in the Cane Creek area preceded the battle. His troops passed through the area on their way to and from the Battle of Guilford Court House. By the beginning of the Lindley Mill Battle, Cornwallis and the British Army had marched out of the state. David Fanning, a notorious Loyalist militia leader, took charge of events in the vacuum left by Cornwallis's departure.

Events before the Battle of Lindley Mill

Events leading up to and surrounding the Battle of Lindley Mill were designed and driven by a controversial historical figure named David Fanning. David Fanning was vilified by Patriots and defended by Loyalists. Understanding David Fanning is pivotal to understanding how the Battle of Lindley Mill came to pass.

David Fanning was born in Virginia in October of 1755. David's father died soon after his birth. Eight years later, David's mother died, leaving him and his sister as orphans. David and his sister were separated and a county justice in Wake County, NC raised him. By his own account, David was not well treated and he ran away at the age of sixteen. After unsuccessfully living alone in the woods, he had to rely on the charity of a family in Orange County, NC. They treated him well and raised him for several years, including teaching him how to read and write.

David also developed a reputation for being able to tame diffi-cult and wild horses, an early indication of his toughness.

David moved to South Carolina when he was 19 years old and became a trader with the Cherokee and Catawba Indians in the Lauren County area. When the revolution began, both sides aggressively recruited in the "Upcountry" area of South Carolina and each resident had to make a decision. As a man, David was best known by his last name and Fanning's decision was made easier when he was assaulted and robbed by a group of Patriots. His vindictive nature quickly led him to swear vengeance with-out mercy to those opposed to the Loyalist cause.

In December of 1775, Thomas Lindley's oldest son, James Lindley also lived in South Carolina's Upcountry. The 40-year old James became a Captain and organized a company of Loyal-ist troops. David Fanning, 20 years old, was a Sergeant in James' company. The area was so divided that James found it necessary to compile a list of who was on which side, as Fanning later recounted:

> "...the first day Of May (1775) Capt. James Lindley
> of Rabern's Creek, sent to me as I was a Sergeant
> of the said company, to have his company warned
> to meet at his house 15 of said month. I did accord-
> ingly, and presented two papers; there were 118
> men signed in favour of the King, also declared to
> defend the same, at the risk of lives and property,
> in July 1775." (Caruthers, 1854, p. 231).

By December of 1775, the unit led by James was engaged in battle. They fought in the "Snow Campaign" at the Battle of Great Cane Break on December 22. Captain Lindley was among 130 prisoners captured and sent to Charleston, but he was soon released. Fanning managed to evade capture by escaping to a nearby Cherokee community before being caught in January of 1776.

Fanning's capture was the first of 14 incarcerations or captures by his enemies during the succeeding three years. Sometimes he was released and other times he made daring escapes. By early 1779, many months of ill treatment in jail and malnutrition from hiding in the woods left him tired, discouraged and ill. Then an event occurred which may have broken Fanning's spirit – the death of James Lindley.

Captain James Lindley and his militia had joined Colonel John Boyd as they marched into Georgia. Patriots commanded by Colonels Andrew Pickens, John Dooley and Elijah Clarke ambushed the Loyalists while they were in camp. This was called the Battle of Kettle Creek and took place in Georgia near Augusta on February 14, 1779. Twenty Loyalists were killed and 22 captured, including James Lindley and his son William. All but five of those captured were let go. William was released, but James and four others were hanged after a quick trial on February 22, 1779.

Fanning's hopes may have been temporarily dashed because he went home and agreed to be neutral in the conflict. His neutrality did not last long. A year later in 1780 when the royal forces captured Charleston on May 12, they began a campaign into the interior of the Carolinas, led by General Cornwallis.

Fanning once again took up arms, following Cornwallis's army as they moved into North Carolina. Although he was only just turning 25 years old that year, Fanning was already battle hardened by his rough upbringing, tough demeanor, ill treatment from the Patriots, and his burning memory of the brutal death of his old captain. Fanning met Cornwall at Cox's Mill, James Lindley's wife's childhood home. David told Cornwallis that he knew the area, knew the people and then proceeded to recruit and raise militia troops loyal to the crown. He sent 500 men to Cornwallis and scouted the area for him before and after the Battle of Guilford Courthouse. Fanning's recruits were eager but mostly without arms, so only 50 were chosen. His vigorous efforts were enough to get him what he truly desired – a command position. After a challenging life, his fortune changed the following year on July 5, 1781 when, at the age of twenty six, he was appointed militia Colonel of the Royal Militia of Chatham and Randolph Counties in North Carolina.

David Fanning lost no time exerting his influence as Cornwallis and the British army left North Carolina. The conflict within North Carolina became more of a civil war as armed bands and small armies, like Fanning's, of Patriot and Loyalist partisans struggled to annihilate one another by hit-and-run attacks; spreading terror among the families and friends of their enemies.

Fanning excelled in this gritty environment, recruiting additional militia troops and participating in 36 skirmishes and battles in central North Carolina. His troops had no support or supply lines, so they raided every household that supported the Patriot cause, taking at will what they wanted and needed. Without regard for unfavorable odds, Fanning attacked any gathering of Patriots as soon as he heard of their whereabouts, frequently marching all day to intersect and surprise his foes. Fanning became feared and hated by his opponents.

Colonel Fanning's promotion and changed circumstances included a resplendent uniform consistent with his rank. Eli Caruthers described Fanning's military genius and reputation at the time of the battle in the following manner:

> During the last three months, his movements had
> been rapid; his plans bold and daring; and in every
> conflict he had come off victorious. Few men, with
> the same amount of force, have ever accomplished
> more in the same length of time (Caruthers, 1854,
> p. 231).

Historian Samuel Ashe summarized Fanning as follows:

> It must be said...that he was one of the boldest
> men, most fertile in expedients and quick in execu-
> tion that ever lived in North Carolina. Had he been
> on the Patriot side, his fame would have been
> more enduring than that of any other partisan of-
> ficer whose memory is now so dear to all patriots
> (Ashe S. A., 1925, p. 93).

In September of 1781, David Fanning, turned his attention to the Haw River Valley. General John Butler, a seasoned

Joseph C. Carlin
43

Brigadier General who had served the local militia since 1770 was Fanning's primary foe in the area. Butler's combat experience included command of the North Carolina militia in some of the most noteworthy battles of the Revolutionary War in the South: Stono Ferry, Camden, and Guilford Court House. In the wake of Continental Army's departure, Fanning received word of Butler's location and put together a large force of troops under his command, then joined up with Scotch-Irish Loyalists led by Colonel Archibald McDugald and Colonel Hector McNeil.

A Bold Plan: Capture the Governor of North Carolina

As David Fanning's troops marched towards Butler's troops at their Haw River encampment, Fanning learned that Governor Thomas Burke was in Hillsborough. A few months earlier, in July, Fanning had made a daring raid into Pittsboro, capturing a large number of prominent Patriots, which he escorted to Wilmington and turned over to the British Army. The thought of capturing the highest-ranking political opponent in the state was too much of a temptation for him to pass up as he describes in his narrative:

> I found myself at the head of 950 men of my own regiment...on the 9th of September I was joined by Col'n McDougald of the loyal militia of Cumberland County, with 200 men; and Hector McNeil, with his party from Bladen of 70 men (Fanning, 1861, p. 34).

According to Fanning's account, his men totaled 1,220, which is considerably larger than estimates from later sources:

> The number engaged on either side is not known with any degree of certainty, but according to the best traditional accounts...the Tories had about six hundred, and the Patriots about three hundred or a little more (Caruthers, 1854, p. 208).

Since the reported Loyalist force at Lindley's Mill was far smaller than the number Fanning reported under his command a few days earlier, he might have selected only the best-armed troops for the attack on Hillsborough.

With 600 to 1200 men, on the morning of September 13, 1781 [September 12, 1781 according to Fanning, but disputed by others], after a night march, reputedly under the cover of a heavy fog, Fanning's forces attacked the village from all sides and captured "all he had sought in this temporary capital of the State" (Fanning, 1861, p. 35). His political booty included the Governor, most of the members of the Governor's Council, members of the General Assembly, a few prominent Patriots, and an armed force of possibly two hundred men. Fanning's capture of the Patriot governor could not be complete until he delivered them to his British superiors in Wilmington.

Unbeknownst to David Fanning, the Patriot Alexander Mebane was able to escape. Mebane promptly headed off to tell General Butler and spread the word among the intensely Patriot residents of the area west of Hillsborough named Hawfields. The news spread rapidly through the Hawfields community that their hated nemesis had captured the Governor. The reaction was swift as they quickly organized and prepared a plan to free their Governor.

Two Roads, But Only One Bridge to Wilmington

General Butler knew all about the exploits of David Fanning, including his Pittsboro triumph. He reasoned that Fanning would march the prisoners directly to Wilmington to deliver them since he had no facility for holding his captives. As maps from the time period confirm, there were only two roads to Wilmington and both converged at the same point: the bridge crossing Cane Creek next to Lindley's Mill.

The first route proceeded due west until it reached Hawfields. There the road turned southwest and crossed the Haw River at the Alamance Creek junction, then continued southwest before splitting into two forks. The right fork headed southwest to Dixon's Mill and Cane Creek Meeting house. The left fork, the route for getting to Wilmington, went southeast directly to Lindley's Mill, the logical location for crossing Cane Creek because of the small bridge.

The second and more direct route proceeded in a southerly direction. Heading southwest from Hillsborough, this route crossed the Haw River at Woody's Ford, just south of Saxapahaw and north of the Haw River intersection with Mary's Creek. After traversing the Haw River, the road continued West to the Spring Meeting House, then turned south and southwest until crossing Stafford's Branch, a tiny tributary, where the small creek fed into the much larger Cane Creek. From that mushy intersection, the path led directly west along Cane Creek for about 200 yards, ending at Lindley's Mill.

Both potential routes merged into one at the bridge adjacent to Lindley's Mill. The citizen-maintained road continued southeast from the bridge, passing through Pittsboro on the way to Fanning's target destination: the city of Wilmington.

General Butler Positions Troops at Stafford's Branch

General Butler figured that Fanning would undoubtedly take the more direct southern route since it avoided passing through Hawfields. The most important part of Fanning's journey for General Butler was the last few hundred yards of the southern route. Along this critical section, the path was bordered on the northern side by a sharp bluff 15 to 20 feet high and on the southern side by the deep waters of Cane Creek. General Butler needed a clear strategic advantage and this section afforded his outnumbered troops the ability to stop Fanning's march since Loyalists would realize that walking between the bluff and the creek would expose them to certain death, forcing a halt to their advance. If the Patriots could stop or delay the march of the Loyalists, then they would have a chance to free the prisoners.

Alternatively, if Fanning's men passed down through Hawfields and approached Lindley Mill from the north along the larger road, General Butler could move his men a few hundred

yards west and attack from a less strategic, but defendable
vantage point beside the road.

Before any of his plans to stop Fanning's forces could take
affect, General Butler needed to get to Lindley's Mill before
Colonel Fanning. Fortunately, the Loyalists helped him out by
delaying their departure. After capturing the Governor and the
other Patriots, which Fanning's autobiography claims was
completed by 7 a.m., the victorious troops failed to leave town
before 12 noon by this same account. As Fanning's soldiers
searched Hillsborough homes for Patriots, they also plundered
for supplies and came across a large stock of whiskey. The
beleaguered troops, tired from their all night march and giddy
from their morning victory, immediately consumed the whisky
and began celebrating. The alcohol driven delay, which Fanning
fails to mention in his autobiographical narrative, gave General
Butler and his troops the time they desperately needed to set
their ambush.

The Loyalists march from Hillsborough was probably less
than orderly, making it necessary for them to halt for the night a
few miles short of the Haw River (Fanning, 1861). The weary
and inebriated troops, sleepless after two hard marches, one
through the night, finally got their rest on the evening of September 13.

Dawn dictated the day's start and they rose and started
moving by 5 a.m. The Loyalists crossed the wide Haw River at
Woody's Ford, about two and one-half miles south of what is
now Saxapahaw and approximately four miles from Lindley's
Mill, using the ferry or wading across the waters, most likely
shallow after the hot, dry summer.

The "roads" of that time, including the northern approach
coming south to Lindley Mill, were built and maintained by the
local citizenry. The route taken by Fanning's militia brought
them past the Spring Meeting House were they veered south and
southwest along a shoulder-width path through the multi-
colored trees and across fields ripe for the fall harvest. The six
hundred Loyalists accompanied by their two hundred prisoners
walked single-file through woods and in small groups across
open fields. As they approached Stafford's Branch, the full

foliage of the dense woods and single file formation obscured their view.

Colonel McNeil and his group of seventy men were charged with providing the front guard, but he had failed to send out any scouts in advance of the column. The only reported teetotaler among the officers was Captain "Sober John" McLean. As a reward for his sobriety, Fanning had astutely put him in charge of the prisoners, who were placed towards the back of the party. At about 9:30 in the morning, "Sober John" notified Colonel Fanning that Colonel McNeil forgot about the scouts. Fanning immediately rode forward along the mile long line, making difficult progress until he caught up with the troops at the front at about ten o'clock in the morning.

As Fanning caught up to and confronted McNeil, they were located close behind the first soldiers as they reached the juncture of Stafford's Branch and Cane Creek. Just as McNeil started to respond to Fanning's query, a volley of musket shots rang out, killing several Loyalists and forcing the rest at the head of the advancing line to drop and lay in the shallow creek bed to protect themselves.

General Butler's surprise worked perfectly, as noted in this historical account:

> As the Tories were crossing the creek, and advanc-
> ing through a hollow of low ground, along which
> the road led, the Patriots from the brow of the hill,
> on the south side of the stream, gave a deliberate
> fire, and with tremendous effect...quite a number
> were killed and wounded as they approached the
> stream, and before any danger was known or ap-
> prehended (Caruthers, 1854, p. 210).

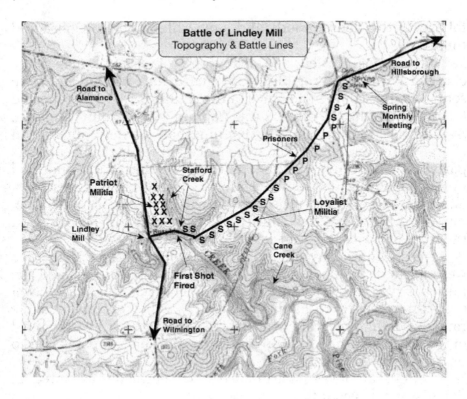

Figure 6 - Battle of Lindley Mill

The Patriots had withheld their fire until the lead men in the advance guard passed the southeastern point of the Plateau. Their line stretched back to the ford of Stafford's Branch and up the hill beyond. Openly exposed to the Patriots' musket fire, McNeil, fresh from being reprimanded by Fanning, took the logical choice and told his men to retreat:

> Colonel McNeill, on seeing so many of his men cut down by the first fire, and perceiving that if they continued to advance, it would be a great sacrifice of life, ordered a retreat;... (Caruthers, 1854, p. 210)

Colonel Archibald McDougal, the commander of the larger regiment of Scots-Irish Highlanders, shamed McNeil for
ordering a retreat, and pushed forward:

> The order was then countermanded and at the first
> fire of the Patriots, five or six balls entered the
> Colonel's [McNeil] body, and he fell on the spot.
> So did several others, and many more were
> wounded (Caruthers, 1854, p. 210).

Several soldiers yelled out that Colonel McNeil was dead,
but Colonel McDougal quickly responded that it was a lie. He
immediately reversed his own ill-timed countermand and pulled
the soldiers back up the path beyond the range of the Patriot
weapons:

> ...For many of the Scotch declared afterwards, that
> had it been known at the time, they would not
> have fired another gun, but would have sought
> safety in any way they could (Caruthers, 1854, p.
> 211).

The Patriot ambush worked exactly as planned and was a
vital part of their strategy. From the vantage point on the hill,
only a small portion of the front guard of the Loyalist army was
able to easily find cover. The entire line of soldiers stalled,
unable to know what was happening or effectively respond. The
ambush was a diversion, planned to coincide with and to facilitate a simultaneous Patriot attack on the rear of the Loyalist
army. The main objective for the Patriots was to free the prisoners, or at least give them a chance to make a break for freedom.

The Battle for the Prisoners

A second group of General Butler's soldiers were hiding
in the woods near Thomas Lindley's house and close to the
Spring Meeting House. As they heard the musket fire, they
moved on the Loyalists near the back of the strung out line,

where the prisoners were held. By simultaneously attacking the front and back of the line, the Patriots hoped to isolate the majority of Loyalist troops in the woods between the two points, providing a temporary advantage for the Patriots.

"Sober John" McLean vigilantly attended to maintaining control over Fanning's prisoners:

> Captain McLean halted his men in the rear and they sat down to rest. On hearing the first fire of the Patriots, Governor Burke and most of the prisoners jumped to their feet and looked about; but the captain told them to be quiet; for if they should attempt to escape they should everyone be shot down; they had to obey (Caruthers, 1854, p. 210).

The immediate reaction of the prisoners must have been exactly what the Patriot attackers desired. The surprised Loyalists were rattled by the prospect of losing their catch and were swift to react:

> A few years ago an old Quaker friend, who appeared to have been well informed on this subject, and whose powers, though he was four score, were unimpaired by age, told me that Colonel McDougal, after he took command, came under great excitement and, to use his own language: 'in a foam of sweat,' proceeded to the house in which the prisoners were then kept, and took an oath that if the Patriots did flank him as they were trying to do, and drive him to extremities, he would put his prisoners all to death, before he would suffer them to be taken from him (Caruthers, 1854, pp. 212-213).

When Colonel McDougal succeeded the fallen Colonel McNeil he became the commander of all the Highlanders, including McLean's company guarding the prisoners. After pulling back the advance guard and securing the front of his line, McDougal and Fanning turned and spurred their horses in the direction of the prisoners. Colonel Fanning sent Colonel McDougal back to check on the prisoners, while Fanning started organizing his troops to retaliate. By the time McDougal reached the prisoners, McLean had already moved and secured the prisoners in the Spring Meeting House that was under construction and unfinished but adequate for containing prisoners.

The Patriots temporary advantage disappeared as the aggressive actions of McLean, McDougal and Fanning took effect. "Sober John" McLean packed the two hundred prisoners into the Spring Meeting House, simultaneously turning it into a prison and a fort. McDougal's threats to massacre the prisoners were shouted to the Patriots as well as to the prisoners. General Butler, learning of the threatened execution of the prisoners, was forced to consolidate his numerically disadvantaged troops back to their position at Stafford's Branch. And then Colonel Fanning onto the offensive:

> I made the necessary preparation to attack the enemy; and after engaging them for four hours they retreated (Fanning, 1861, p. 35).

Four Hours of Musket Fire

The patriot position above the intersection of Stafford's Branch and Cane Creek, as confirmed by musket balls found in the slope, was effective for halting the Loyalists. Fanning was able to figure out the weakness of the Patriot's position. The north side of the steep hill leveled out at the top and created a plateau. By counterattacking from the north, Fanning's troops turned around the Patriots' advantage as the Patriots became pinned between his advancing troops and the steep decline behind them above the path beside Cane Creek. Meanwhile, McDougal's front guard troops regrouped and chose a vantage point on their side of Stafford's Branch about six feet high. From this position, they fired directly at the Patriots on the higher slope. The effective range of 50-70 yards for muskets made the

30-yard gap between the two groups lethal and deaths were sustained by both sides.

The Patriots were forced to fight two close range battles on their north and east flanks. Over the course of four hours, the Patriots fought for their lives, unwilling to give up and join the 200 prisoners Fanning already had. Each militia attacked the other, but both sides managed to hold their ground. General Butler then ordered a retreat, but:

> ...Col. Robert Mebane got before them, and by ar-
> gument and remonstrance, so far inspired them
> with his own heroic spirit that enough of them re-
> turned to renew the battle and keep the ground
> (Caruthers, 1854, p. 212).

Fighting continued until the Patriots started to run out of powder, leading Colonel Mebane to personally supply his troops, filling his hat with black powder and distributing its contents. Despite determined efforts on each side, the casualties eventually became overwhelming:

> Between the foot of the hill and the creek, the dead
> and dying were strewed about in every direction,
> some of them lying in the water. One of the Scotch
> companies, the one under the command of Capt.
> Archibald M'Kay had six killed on the ground and
> twenty-six wounded; some other companies suf-
> fered equally as much and hardly any of them es-
> caped entirely (Caruthers, 1854, p. 214).

The Scots-Irish Highlanders in the Loyalist front guard probably took the brunt of the deaths. Tradition tells of a mass grave containing thirty-four dead buried in one grave. The location of the grave is not known, but is most likely adjacent to the critical point of initial impact: where Stafford's Branch and Cane Creek intersect.

The two-to-one ratio by which the Loyalists outnumbered the Patriots was offset by the favorable position held by the

Patriots high on their Plateau. There they were able to keep their entire force together in one body, fighting a defensive battle. The Loyalists were able to attack from two sides, but not able to breach the steep hill and held back from attacking too aggressively across the plateau for fear that the prisoners would be left exposed behind them. The Loyalists guarding the prisoners also had to be constantly vigilant, not knowing if there would be another raid on their fortified position.

The Battle's Conclusion

Just as it appeared that Colonel Mebane's Patriot forces would be overwhelmed, Colonel David Fanning became a casualty when he was seriously wounded and removed from the battlefield:

> At the conclusion of this action, I received a shot in my left arm, which broke the bone in several pieces; my loss of blood was so great, that I was taken off my horse, and led to a secret place in the woods. I then sent Lieutenant Woleston to my little army, for Col'n Arch McDugald, and Major John Rains and Lt. Col'n Arch McKay, to take command...I also desired that Major Rains return as soon as he could leave Col. McDugald; as I thought he might be able to save me from the hands of my enemies (Fanning, 1861, p. 36).

The Loyalists, tired after four hours of fighting, many probably still feeling the effects from the previous day's whiskey, then lost their will to continue fighting. The Patriots, having run low on ammunition and also fatigued from fighting on two fronts for four hours, took advantage of the cessation of musket shot and retreated to Alamance Creek. The Loyalists proceeded to finally cross the bridge at Cane Creek, making camp that night not too far south before continuing on to Wilmington with their prisoners the following day.

Once he realized that the Loyalists were not following, General Butler reorganized his remaining troops, resupplied those willing and able to continue, and made preparations to pursue the enemy. Most likely their pursuit did not occur until the next day.

The Loyalists did not have to march far before they entered the Deep River Valley (south of where present day highway U.S. 1 crosses the Haw and Deep Rivers), an area sympathetic to their cause and loyal to the Crown. The pursuit by General Butler and his Patriots was annoying to the Loyalists, but not effective since they were never able to again threaten Loyalist control of the prisoners. Colonel Duncan Ray of the Royal Anson County Militia accepted transfer of the prisoners and conducted them safely to Wilmington.

Meanwhile, finding out about Fanning's injury, a small group of Patriot militia under Captain William O'Neal returned to the battle area and searched, but could not locate Fanning. Fanning's account states that he was initially left with only three men, then another seventeen showed up four days later. Fanning's wound was serious and he was not able to sit up for twenty-four days, but he survived to fight additional battles.

The Aftermath

Patriot and Loyalist dead were everywhere, strewn across Thomas Lindley's property following the battle. Both sides left behind many seriously wounded soldiers, unable to move from where they were injured. After the cessation of the battle, the local residents, primarily Quakers, began to treat the wounded. Doctor John Pyle, a staunch Loyalist, was one of the first to arrive on the scene. He faithfully administered medical assistance to the many wounded soldiers on both sides.

Fanning estimated that his side killed 27 and seriously wounded another sixty. The Patriots buried 24 and had 90 seriously wounded. This combined total equals 51 dead and 150 seriously wounded. The largest group, previously mentioned, was the thirty-four men buried in one grave by the Society of Friends. The community's effort must have involved all the local families and been spread out among almost every home to be able to attend to 150 seriously wounded and simultaneously bury 51 men.

The Battle of Lindley's Mill must really be regarded as a civil war between two local militia groups; neighbor against neighbor, brother against brother...a bleak foreshowing of later Civil War battles also fought for control of North Carolina. The Battle of Lindley's Mill ranks as one of the most important Revolutionary War battles in the state. The control of North Carolina seemed vital in September of 1781 because no one could imagine at that moment that a month later General Charles Cornwallis and the British Army would surrender in Yorktown, Virginia and bring an end to the war.

The Battle of Lindley's Mill ended up yielding only a one-day delay for the Loyalists as they journeyed to Wilmington. The Patriots failed to free Governor Burke or any of the prisoners. Fanning's brilliant coup when he captured so many high-value prisoners at Hillsborough was the real victory. The Patriots were able to pull together an effective military strategy on short notice that, with only one-half the numerical strength of their enemy, allowed them to execute two simultaneous surprise attacks that could have freed the prisoners. The swift response of the Loyalist Militia allowed them to retain control after the initial surprise. The Patriot's subsequent stand, holding off the much larger force at point-blank range during four continuous hours of musket exchange, followed by a safe withdrawal without surrendering, must be admired. David Fanning might have summarized it as "A delay, nothing more" except that he joined 200 other soldiers who received lethal or critical wounds.

Death of Thomas Lindley, Sr.

Unfortunately, the story did not end there for Thomas Lindley. As previously mentioned, several families, including the Lindley family were tragically split with sympathies on both sides and in the middle. As a result, father was pitted against son and brother against brother. Thomas Lindley was 76 years of age when the battle occurred on his land and he died the same day. His death was as a result of a heart attack or stroke, most likely brought on by the shock of seeing these events transpire on the land on which he had put his hopes, raised his family and diligently cultivated for 28 years.

After the battle the women tended to the wounded from both sides at Thomas Lindley's home, the homes of his neighbors, and on the floor of the Spring Monthly Meeting House, which at that time was under construction. Lumber for the ceiling was stacked on the floor and became blood stained from the wounds. The lumber was put into place without removing the bloodstains and remained visible on the ceiling as a reminder of the battle for many years (Wilson).

Will for Thomas Lindley, Sr.

Whereas I, Thomas Lindley of the County Orange in North Carolina being far advanced in years, be of a sound mind and memory and well knowing the uncertainty of life, and certainty of death at one time or other, do think it's mindful to leave behind me the following lines, as my last will and testament. That is to say principally and first of all, I promise my soul to the Lord, and my body to the earth to be dutifully buried, at the direction of my executor, hereafter named, and as touching such worldly substance with which I am now proposing to leave bequeathed and disown of the same in manner of form following.

First, it is my will that all my just debts of funeral expenses be fully paid and satisfied. I give and bequeath unto my beloved Ruth Lindley the sum of 100 pounds together with all my household furniture except one featherbed and furniture, and the privilege of the new end of the house I now dwell in, likewise a sufficient maintenance in new pay provisions and her firewood cut and drawn to her need, also keeping for one horse and two cows and it is my will that she...[section not readable]...being part of the track I now live on, to be laid off for him in the following manner, beginning at a red Oak, the North West corner of the whole tract, running three 33 chains 3 yards and 2 feet south to a stake and East 60 chains to a stake. Then north 33 chains 3 yards and 2 feet to a post oak then West to the first station, to him the said William Lindley his heirs and assigns, forever. I give and bequeath unto my daughter Catharine White the sum of 20 pounds to her and to her heirs forever. I also give and bequeath unto all my other children Thomas Lindley, Ruth Hadley, William Lindley, John Lindley, Eleanor Maris and Deborah Newlin, to each and every of them, the sum of 20 pounds, to them and their heirs forever.

I also give and bequeath unto my son Jonathan Lindley the remainder of the tract of land or plantation whereon I now do dwell, to him his heirs and assigns forever, and it is my will that he shall assign his mother the above privileges which I have hereby bequeathed to her, I also give onto my son Jonathan Lindley my Mill and one featherbed and furniture, and it is my will that all the legacies herein before mentioned shall be paid to each and every of the above mentioned legatees within one year after my decease, I give and bequeath unto Thomas Lindley, son of James Lindley Senior the sum of 10 pounds to be paid to him within one year after my decease, I give and bequeath unto my grandson Thomas Lindley son of Thomas Lindley the sum of 10 pounds to be paid to him when he arrives to the age of 21 years I give and bequeath unto my grandson Thomas Lindley son of William Lindley the sum of 10 pounds to be paid to him when he arrives to the age of 21 years, to them their heirs and assigns forever, I also give and bequeath unto Friends Spring Meeting two acres of land where the meeting house lays, to them and their heirs forever, and it is my will that all of any remainder or over plus of my personal estate (if any there be), after the above-mentioned legacies is paid shall be equally divided amongst my children then and then alike and if any of my children should die before the legacies become due, then it is my will that the legacy bequeathed to the child so dying to be divided equally amongst my surviving children, and if either of my grandchildren legacies herein mentioned should die before he or they arrive to the age of 21 years then it is my will that the father of such child so dying shall have the said child support.

And lastly I do hereby nominate constitute and appoint my sons William and Jonathan Lindley whole and sole and executors to this my last will and testament, hereby making void all other wills by me made or that may hereafter appear in my name. Ratifying and confirming this and no other to be my last will and testament.

In witness whereof I have hereunto set my hand and seal this 15th day of the third month in the year of our Lord 1780.

[signed]

Thomas Lindley, Sr.

(Orange County NC Clerk of Court)

Summary of the terms of the will

Ruth Lindley, Wife

> *100 pounds,*
> *household furniture,*
> *maintenance pay, firewood,*
> *one horse, two cows*

William Lindley

> *Acreage 33.3.2 x 60 chains totals 2000, divid-*
> *ed by 10 equals 200 acres*

Jonathan Lindley

> *Remainder of tract of land where Thomas, Sr.*
> *lived*
> *The Grist Mill,*
> *one featherbed and furniture*

Children: Catharine White, Thomas Lindley, Ruth
Hadley, William Lindley, John Lindley, Eleanor
Maris, Deborah Newlin

> *20 pounds each*

Grandchildren: Thomas, son of James; Thomas,
son of Thomas; Thomas, son of William

> *10 pounds each when they turn 21*

Friends Spring Meeting

> *2 acres of land where the meetinghouse lays*

Eight of Thomas Lindley's ten children are directly referred to in his will. James, who was already deceased, is indi-
rectly referred to in mentioning his son Thomas. Simon, who
died in 1760, is also not mentioned. Thomas, Sr. had a total of
six sons. Using some speculation, he probably had already given
200 acres of land to James, Thomas, and John prior to his
death, leaving 400 acres, which he allocated in the will - 200 to
William, aged 38 and (unspecified) about 200 to Jonathan, aged
25. Jonathan got the gristmill as well, with instructions to
provide for the maintenance of his mother. While this speculation helps with the expectation of an equitable distribution, it
appears without more information that Jonathan may have
come out with the best result from these transactions.

The emphasis on land ownership during the life and
death of Thomas Lindley reflected the values of the time. Land
ownership was a key measure of success for colonial and post-
revolutionary farmers and orchard growers. Thomas Lindley, Sr.

owned at least 1,000 acres and possibly as much as 2,000 acres. During his life and in his will he helped to insure that his children were landowners, thereby helping them get a head start in being able to support themselves and their large families.

Immediate Ancestors

This section transitions from J. Van Lindley's early ancestors to his immediate forefathers - his Great Grandfather, Grandfather, and Father. These men were concerned about land - acquisition, preparation, cultivation, and the profits derived from hard work. They were ambitious and eager to continue defining the American dream. They were also prolific progenitors. Success may have been combined in these two concerns, because they each seemed to be focused on buying 1000 acres, working it with a large family, then giving off pieces to their male heirs. To succeed at their ambitions, they had to take advantage of the opening of inexpensive lands as expansion continued in the U.S. As we examine these 3 men, we will focus on their land, wealth and families. To set the stage for this examination, we can look back at the track record of Thomas Lindley, Sr. He was able to buy about 1,000 acres and pass it on to his children. Thomas, Sr. had 11 children and 103 grandchildren.

Thomas Lindley, Junior, 1st Great Grandfather

Thomas Lindley, Jr., the Great Grandfather of J. Van Lindley, was born in London Grove, Pennsylvania on August 7, 1740. He moved with his family to North Carolina in the mid 1750's. Sometime in late 1758 or early 1759, at the age of 18 or 19, he married Sarah Evans, a 15-year-old neighbor whose family were not Quakers. However, Sarah's stepfather was Hugh Laughlin, the partner of Thomas, Sr. in the gristmill later known as Lindley's Mill. Sarah's father Owen died when she was 3 years old. Her mother subsequently married Hugh and then moved with him from Delaware to North Carolina. Since Sarah was not a Quaker, Thomas, Jr. was "disowned" by the congregation. This was a common practice at the time and a means for encouraging the faithful to choose mates from within the body of believers. The Quakers admitted Thomas, Jr. and his 15-year-old bride back into the congregation on May 1, 1759, also following the common practice of the time.

Thomas, Jr. began accumulating land at the age of 25 years old on August 13, 1765 with a purchase of 300 acres from his father (Bennett Vol. VIII, P. 41). He continued buying land in the Cane Creek, Little Cane Creek, South Fork of Cane Creek, Terrell Creek and Eno River areas. The land records from that time period are not complete, but his land holdings were between 2,000 and 3,000 acres during his life. He was a substantial owner of property, buying land from unrelated neighbors and from the newly formed State of North Carolina before dividing it up and selling the majority of his holdings to his children. The primary concentration of his land was in the Cane Creek area, with about 500 acres near the Eno River or Terrell Creek, but most of it within a 10-mile radius. Based upon available records, Thomas, Jr. sold 200-400 acre tracts of land to his sons during his lifetime. He bought out his wife's family and became a partner in the gristmill, selling it, along with 300 acres of land in 1811 for $5,000, and then buying it back with his son William in 1825 without the land for $4,000. He sold his undivided half of the partnership to William in 1833 prior to his death.

Tragedy continued to strike the Lindley family in the immediate years following the deaths of James Lindley and Thomas Lindley, Sr. In November of 1782, the brother-in-law of Thomas, Jr., George Maris, died. A few months later, Thomas, Jr.'s sister Eleanor Lindley Maris died. The death of these two parents left seven children parentless. As detailed in the Orange County court records of 1785, the seven children were adopted by the remaining Lindley family members, with each family taking one or two of the children. A few years after Eleanor died, Thomas, Jr.'s brother William also died, leaving a widow.

The impact of these deaths included a lot of legal work for both Thomas, Jr. and Jonathan. They had to work with the courts on the wills, estates, and children custody issues. Administration of the estates also included selling and distributing property and paying off debts. John Lindley, the only other living brother, was not a participant in any of these activities, other than receiving his share of his father's estate.

Thomas, Jr. and Sarah were married for 37 years until Sarah's death in 1796. Together they had eleven children, and 127 grandchildren. The staggering math of multiple generations of large families - Thomas, Sr., Thomas, Jr., and (as we'll see next) Aaron - each having over 100 grandchildren for several generations, with life spans averaging between 60 to 80 years, excluding early deaths, has some interesting implications. First, it must have been difficult to know all of the grandchildren. Thomas Jr. lived until he was 93, dying in 1833 in North Carolina; having lived in his adopted state for 80 years. By the time Thomas Jr. died, he must have had over 250 living descendants. Second, the family tradition of repeatedly using the same names left many Thomas's, James's, Jonathan's, John's, etc. The inclusion of middle names became more common as the 1800's progressed and reduced the confusion. Third, the potential dilution of family wealth is also hard to ignore with so many family members. The Lindley families were primarily farmers living in an environment where many inexpensive laborers were needed, the price of land was relatively inexpensive, and huge fortunes could potentially be created in short periods of time. Because of these dynamics, along with Quakers refusing to participate in owning slaves, having many children made a certain amount of logical and economical sense.

Thomas Jr. lived about 3 miles south of Lindley Mill, off of the present day Lindley Mill Road. Eight years following the death of his first wife, he married Marjorie Piggott Buckingham, a widow. According to one tradition, they took in and raised a "colored" boy, the son of Sandy Burnett, a Revolutionary War drummer. The boy named his own son Thomas Burnett after Thomas Lindley. Thomas gave two acres of land for the South Fork Friends Church in 1800 and it was confirmed in his will below. Both he and Marjorie are buried at that church.

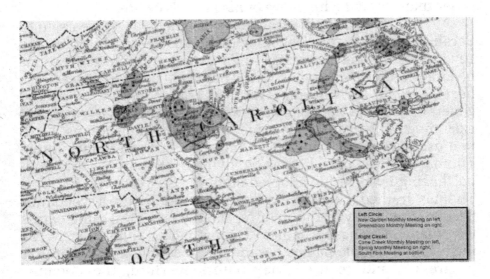

Figure 7 - Location of Quaker Monthly Meetings

Settlement of the Estate of Thomas Lindley, Jr.

Dr. James Lindley, Executor in account current, with the estate of THOMAS LINDLEY, Deceased, Cr.

Be paid Thomas Stout for walnut coffin - 50 cents
Court charges on for wills - $1.50
Paid for crying sale - $1.00
Paid Sarah Lindley - $12.00
Paid James Lindley - $7.55
Exp. paid Robert Andrew - $1.15
Paid William McBane - $1.92
Paid William Lindley - $1.60

SUBTOTAL - $27.22

5% on $108.805 on receipts - $5.44
5% on $27.22 expenditures - $1.36

SUBTOTAL - $34.02

Deduct expenditures as above - $108.805

Balance due the estate - $34.02

SUBTOTAL - $74.785

The will for Thomas Lindley, Jr.

To all Christian people to whom these presents may come, greeting.

Whereas, I, Thomas Lindley of the County of Chatham and State of North Carolina, calling to mind the uncertainty of time and the great certainty of death, DO this the 24th day of the second month in the year of our Lord one thousand eight hundred and thirty three, make and publish this as my last will and testament in manner and form as followeth:

It is my will and I order that my boddy be decently buried. Secondly that my just debts be paid. I will then bequeath unto my daughter, Sarah Lindley, the plantation I live on lying on the north side and west side of the Creek, supposed to contain about one hundred and sixty acres which I will to her airs and assigns forever, and it is my will that she shall have all the stock that I own and all the property that is in my house, piaza and little room except my clock and wearing apparel. It is my will also that she shall have all my ploughs and gears and farming tools and all the corn fodder and oats that I have on hand and to have the ensuing crop of wheat and corn. It is my will that my son, John Lindley, shall have the plantation whereon he now liveth lying on the south and east side of the creek, except two acres where the meeting house now stands which belongs to the FRIENDS of that meeting as long as the meeting is kept up, supposed to contain one hundred and eighty acres of land which I will to him, his heirs and assigns for-

ever, and it is my will that she shall have my wag-
gon and one half of my wearing apperel, and my
son, Joshua Lindley, the other half. It is my will
that the quarter section of land that I have lying in
the state of Indiana, Green County, be divided
among my children one half to my heirs out there
and the other half to come to my heirs here. What
remains of my personal property that is not willed,
it is my will that it shall be equally divided among
my children viz: James Lindley and my grandson,
Jonathan Lindley, my daughter Mary Braxton and
my son, Joshua Lindley. Lastly, I constitute and
appoint my sons, James Lindley and my grandson
Jonathan Lindley, and David Lindley, my whole
and sole executors, in trust for the purpose herein
mentioned, David Lindley, to the part of my estate
which lies in the state of Indiana. In witness
whereof, I have hereunto set my hand and seal the
day and year above written.

Witness present
Thos. Lindley
Wm. Lindley
Hannah Lindley

(Seal)
Thos. Lindley

Summary of the terms of the will

Sarah Lindley, wife

> *160 acres, plus the house*
> *farm implements*
> *corn, oats, and crops*

John Lindley, son

> *180 acres, less 2 acres for Friends Meeting*
> *House = 178 acres*

the wagon
1/2 of wearing apparel

Joshua Lindley, son

1/2 of wearing apparel

Indiana Heirs

80 Acres in Indiana, Green County

North Carolina Heirs

80 Acres in Indiana, Green County

James Lindley, son
Jonathan Lindley, grandson
Mary Braxton, daughter
Joshua Lindley, son

Each gets a 1/4 share of the personal property

Executors:

James Lindley, son
Jonathan Lindley (grandson)
David Lindley, son

Not mentioned (except David as executor) and re-ceiving only a small share of the land in Green County, Indiana:

Owen Lindley, son
William Lindley, son
Thomas Lindley III, son
Aaron Lindley, son
David Lindley, son

The remaining records for Thomas, Jr. are not as clear or robust as they were for his father. We do know that when Thomas, Sr. died Thomas, Jr. was 41 years old. The only conclusive census record for Thomas, Jr. is from the 1830 census when he is listed as living in Pittsboro, Chatham County, NC. At that point he is correctly listed as being 90 years old and identifies himself as "Thomas Lindley, Senior." Two other Thomas Lindley entries show up in the same census, also living in Pittsboro, but each of them is much younger (United States Government 1830). There is a Thomas Lindley, "Sen." in Paoli, Orange County, Indiana in 1820 listed as being in the oldest category "over 45"(United States Government 1820). Since six of his eleven children died in Indiana, and the oldest two in Paoli, there is reason to believe this was a valid location for him that year. There were no records for him found in census searches for 1810. The briefest of descriptions of the life of Thomas Lindley, Jr. is that he was born in 1740, lived for 93 years and died in 1833. By the time of his death it appears likely that he had followed many other settlers in moving to Indiana, but later returned to the town of Pittsboro in his native state of North Carolina, where he lived at the time of his death. He is listed in each available census as living next to other Lindleys, most likely his children.

Aaron Lindley, Grandfather

The paternal grandfather of J. Van Lindley was named Aaron Lindley. Aaron was born in 1768 and was the third child of eleven children with eight brothers and two sisters.

Aaron married Phoebe McPherson at the age of 19 on February 13, 1787 in Chatham County, NC. The Quakers disowned Aaron and Phoebe on February 9, 1789 for marrying outside of the faith. They were reinstated and tradition holds that Aaron was a Cane Creek Quaker and that, before moving to Indiana, they owned a large amount of acreage from Chestnut Hill north, east of the Meachum Lindley home. Together they had 13 children. Their twelfth child was J. Van Lindley's father - Joshua Lindley.

Figure 8 - Aaron Lindley

Unlike prior ancestors, Aaron's father Thomas, Jr., as mentioned above, lived until he was 93 years old. This stopped the concentration of wealth passing that had occurred to that point due to the prior ancestor's short lives, quick fortunes, and relatively few heirs. There is no surviving record of Aaron purchasing land from his father, but he did receive some family assistance in his wealth building with his first purchase at age 26 of 135 acres for 15 pounds. His father was the executor of the estate of Aaron Jones and Aaron Lindley purchased the land from the estate. As reflected in Chatham County records, Aaron Lindley purchased at least 774 acres within the county and sold 1,956 acres between 1792 and 1835. Since the records are not complete, it appears he owned a total of about 2,000 acres, and then sold all of it to his sons. In 1834, just before liquidating most of his North Carolina property, Aaron purchased 320 additional acres in Indiana.

Aaron's real estate interest in Indiana was part of a large wave of settlers that included one-third of the east coast population. They travelled to the "West" (today the "Midwest") to take advantage of an Act of Congress passed on April 24, 1820 entitled: "An Act making further provision for the sale of the Public Lands." This act eliminated the purchase of public land in the United States on credit. It also reduced the minimum size of a tract from 160 to 80 acres, required a down payment of $100 and reduced the price from $1.65 to $1.25 per acre. This new, lower price made it possible for settlers (with cash) to move to the West (Indiana, Illinois, and Missouri) (Wikipedia).

In 1828 the northwest quarter of the State of Indiana was organized into the Crawfordsville District. A land auction office was located in the town of Crawfordsville, Indiana. The lands were sold in 80-acre tracts, half tracts (40 acres), or less if the settler would pay the surveying fee. A law followed this on May 28, 1830 that permitted any Indian tribe to trade its land for lands beyond the Mississippi. During the summer of 1833, and later, government agents were busy in Indiana buying up land and transporting the Indians to the West (Esarey).

July of 1832 found Joshua Lindley, Aaron's son, and J. Van Lindley's father, recorded as the first Lindley to buy land in the Morgan County area known as "Township 13 North, Range One West." The land Joshua bought was southwest of the modern day city of Indianapolis and immediately northwest of the modern day town of Monrovia. Joshua purchased 2 tracts of about 80 acres each that year, followed by a third 80-acre purchase in 1833. When Joshua bought the third tract of land, his brother David Lindley also bought himself a large 160-acre tract on the same day. The two brothers must have sent home glowing reports because their father Aaron, with three more sons (James, Edward, and Owen) and a son-in-law Joshua Hadley arrived in 1834. The Lindley family collectively purchased 1640 acres between 1832 and 1838 within a 2-3 square mile area northwest of the town of Monrovia, Indiana. The Lindley family was a part of history as their experience was repeated many times across the Midwest and western parts of the United States during the 1800's until all inhabitable areas were settled.

Aaron and his family followed in the footsteps of the previous Lindley patriarchs by buying inexpensive land in the hopes of clearing it and converting it to crop producing farmland. His purchases were recorded on documents, which were all signed by the then sitting President of the United States (Bureau of Land Management):

> 80 acres "the West Half, of the South West Quarter of Section Three in township thirteen North, Range One West in the District of Lands subject to sale at Crawfordsville, Indiana." The document was signed on September 16, 1834, Certificate 18003. Morgan County. [$100 estimated price]

> 77 71/100 acres "the East Half, of the North West Quarter of Section Two in township thirteen North, Range One West in the District of Lands subject to sale at Crawfordsville, Indiana." The document was signed on September 16, 1834, Certificate 18004. Morgan County. [$97 estimated price]

> 75 41/100 acres "the East Half of the North West Quarter of Section Five in township thirteen North, Range One West in the District of Lands subject to sale at Crawfordsville, Indiana." The document was signed on October 14, 1834, Certificate 19710. Morgan County. [$94 estimated price]

> 75 04/100 acres "the West Half of the North West Quarter of Section Five in township thirteen North, Range One West in the District of Lands subject to sale at Crawfordsville, Indiana." The document was signed on October 14, 1834, Certificate 19711. Morgan County. [$94 estimated price]

> The total of Aaron's land acreage and estimated prices paid equal 308.16 acres for about $385.

One of Aaron's sons who did not move to Morgan County, but instead moved north of Indianapolis in Hamilton County, was also named Aaron. The younger Aaron was a strong abolitionist, a blacksmith and a gunsmith. He purchased eleven hundred acres of land in Hamilton County and made guns that were used during the Civil War. Aaron's lands became a station on the underground railway where runaway slaves took refuge in their journey north. He had an old barn with a trap door where he hid the slaves in the cellar of the barn. When night fell he would take them further north in his wagon. He was never caught assisting them (Wikipedia).

The last mention of the elder Aaron is when he is listed in the 1850 U.S. Census in Brown, Morgan, Indiana (United States Government 1850) living with his son James and daughter-in-law Ruth. Aaron, aged 83, and his grandson Calvin, aged 21, are each listed as having the occupation "sadler." James is a recorded as a farmer with an appraised property value of $4,830, which was an above average amount of land owned for the immediate area where he lived. The average price of farmland in Indiana in 1850 had risen to $5.17, implying that James' land holdings were about 934 acres (Wallis). James had only purchased 240 acres on his own from the government, so his land holdings may have included his father's 320 acres and all or part of Joshua's land (as we shall later see, Joshua had moved back to North Carolina by this time). Aaron, by this advanced age, was no longer able to work the land himself and most likely had his land in his son James' custodial care by 1850.

Aaron died on April 22, 1853 in Morgan, Indiana at the age of 85 and is buried in West Union Cemetery in Monroe Township, east of Monrovia.

1850 Census

The United States Census of 1850 (United States Government 1850) was a key event for genealogists. Census records were kept every ten years in the United States beginning soon after the Revolutionary War in 1790. The first 6 censuses only listed the head of household by name. The remaining columns were divided into groupings like "Boys (or Girls)-Under age 5," "Boys 5-10," etc. Beginning in 1850, each individual was listed along with age, sex, occupation (if any), value of property (if any), place of birth, and other information, which changed from census to census. Since the 1850 census gave historians and genealogists the first chance to pinpoint exactly who was living where and with whom, it justifies a more thorough analysis.

By 1850, most of the Lindley families had moved out of Pennsylvania and were located in North Carolina, South Carolina and Indiana. The focus of the study is limited to the paternal side of the family, specifically those with the Lindley last name. While this leaves out probably one-half of the relatives, it still gives insight into the movements of the family and reasons for these movements. A study of all people in Indiana collected by the 1850 Census with the Lindley last name revealed a total of 391 individuals. Each of the Lindley families was then cross-referenced to an extensive genealogical database of descendants of James Lindley (the ancestor who came from Ireland to Pennsylvania in 1713). There were 237 Lindley families in the family tree and each were individually tagged and traced to confirm their lineage to Thomas Lindley, Sr. (The same analysis was done of Chatham County, NC and the results are included parenthetically.) The results were then grouped by Thomas, Sr.'s sons, then grandsons, as follows:

John had 35 descendants, with land value of $10,750

James

> *Green, Howard - 12 (the town of Green in Howard County, 12 descendants)*
>
> *Howard, Howard - 5*
>
> *Jackson, Howard - 18*

Jonathan had 25 descendants with land value of $13,500:

Jonathan

Paoli, Orange - 5

Thomas

Paoli, Orange - 6

William

Monroe, Howard - 5

Paoli, Orange - 9

Thomas, Jr. had 173 descendants, with land value of $67,790:

Aaron (plus 30 in Chatham County, NC worth $7,800)

Brown, Morgan -12

Monroe, Morgan - 23

Washington, Hamilton - 8

David

Paoli, Orange - 15

James L. (plus 23 in Chatham County, NC worth $1,550)

Liberty, Parke - 13

John

Fulton, Fountain - 8

Liberty, Parke - 6

Jonathan

Salem, Washington - 3

Liberty, Parke - 16

Joshua (6 worth $1,000)

Owen

Paoli, Orange - 22

Thomas III

Paoli, Orange - 2

Fulton, Fountain - 13

William

Paoli, Orange - 14

Orleans, Orange - 16

William had 3 descendants, with land value of
$5,000

Washington, Washington - 3

The split between the 59 relatives staying in North Carolina and the 237 residing in Indiana (remembering that this is only the male side of the family) shows that the motivation to move was great. Economically, the total family wealth listed in the census divided by family members (average wealth per person) came up to $411 for those who went to Indiana and $175 for those who stayed in North Carolina. While this is a small sample, the lure of wealth creation appears to be real. Despite propagating huge families, the economics of buying the inexpensive land and working it with inexpensive (family) labor seems to have worked. Subsequent transportation changes with the advent of the train, plus the industrial revolution, and the lack of further land grant areas changed the incentives for having large families. However, for the period from 1800 to 1850, the Lindley family seems to have understood how to take advantage of their situation and create wealth. The total sum of combined wealth of the male side of the family, just based upon reported land value, for family members in both states is $107,340. This is greatly in excess of the 1,000 pounds James Lindley left in 1726. Based upon land prices averaging $5.17/acre in 1850, this implies they owned 20,762 acres. To put this in perspective, in 2008 the average price of land in Indiana was $2,693/acre. Multiplying it out, this means the total comes out to $55.9 million in 2004 dollars (Dobbins). Even with 300 family members, that sum would insure a relatively wealthy lifestyle.

The second conclusion we can draw is that families stuck together. All the descendants of John lived in the same county. The same goes for William and for James, except 5 who lived near Thomas, Jr.'s descendants. Even the numerous descendants of Thomas, Jr. ended up being broken down into five large county groups: Orange, IN - 69, Chatham, NC - 53, Morgan, IN - 36, Parke, IN - 35 and Fountain, IN - 24. The exception to this is the 16 remaining descendants who were spread across 3 Indiana counties.

A third conclusion regarding J. Van Lindley and his father is that they were descended from the part of the family that accumulated the most descendants and the most wealth as a group for several generations - Thomas Sr., Thomas, Jr., and Aaron (Aaron's group was worth about $26,000 followed by brother William at $20,000). The emphasis on this pecuniary focus is several: first, the data is available, second, the intent is on trying to find out what was important in their lives, and third, from an anthropological and behavioral standpoint, it demonstrates that there was a certain amount of hereditary expectation of success leading up to the birth of Joshua and then his son J. Van Lindley. Whether it was genetically passed on, behaviorally modeled, or a string of coincidentally strong leaders, the pattern was clearly established.

The final comment added to this section is that Jonathan Lindley, the youngest son of Thomas, Sr. (not in the direct line to J. Van Lindley, but a close relative), was one of the early settlers in Indiana. Jonathan arrived with his family in 1811 and, according to one of his descendants who wrote a book about Jonathan, the family tradition held that he moved to Indiana in 1811 with $100,000 in gold. Jonathan laid out the town of Paoli in 1816, owning 4/13 of the city at the time (Esarey 242). Also in 1816, a writer named David Thomas wrote a book Travels through the Western Country in the Summer of 1816 (Thomas). He mentions meeting J. Lindley and staying with him on July 2-3, 1816, relaying that Jonathan had moved there 5 years prior and was at the time living in the "wilderness" and that during the War of 1812, Jonathan's house was part of a small community that formed the frontier (H. Lindley). Jonathan subsequently served on the original board of 7 trustees that established the University of Indiana and selected the site of Bloomington, Indiana for its campus in 1820, prior to his death in 1828 at the age of 71 (Wylie).

Joshua Lindley, Father

J. Van Lindley's father, Joshua Lindley, was born in 1804 in Chatham County, NC (an area that was subsequently changed to southern Alamance County). Joshua was the twelfth of thirteen children.

At the age of 27 Joshua left his home state of North Carolina. He was granted a certificate from Spring MM on November 26, 1831 to move to Duck Creek MM in Indiana for the purpose of marrying. He married Judith Henley on February 8, 1832 at Walnut Ridge meetinghouse in Rush County, Indiana (just East of Indianapolis) (Hinshaw). By mid-July of the same year he purchased almost 160 acres in Morgan County, Indiana and on January 7, 1833 he was granted a certificate and then was received on April 17, 1833 at White Lick MM in Morgan County, Indiana (Southeast of Indianapolis) (Hinshaw). He was one of the pioneer settlers in Morgan County, as emphasized by the fact that the 1830 census listed only 579 inhabitants. As a comparison, the same year, further south, Orange County, IN had 5,909, Fountain County had 7,644, and Parke County had 7,534 inhabitants. Joshua added an additional 80 acres during the summer of 1833, completing his total Indiana land holdings to include slightly less than 240 acres, as described in government documents (Bureau of Land Management):

> 78 71/100 acres "the West Half, of the North East Quarter of Section Three in township Thirteen North, Range One West in the District of Lands subject to sale at Crawfordsville, Indiana." The document was signed on July 10, 1832, Certificate 15354. Morgan County. [$98 estimated price]
>
> 78 93/100 acres "the East Half, of the North West Quarter of Section Three in township Thirteen

North, Range One West in the District of Lands
subject to sale at Crawfordsville, Indiana." The
document was signed on July 10, 1832, Certificate
15355. Morgan County. [$98 estimated price]

78 93/100 acres "the West Half of the North West
Quarter of Section Three in township Thirteen
North, Range One West in the District of Lands
subject to sale at Crawfordsville, Indiana." The
document was signed on June 8, 1833, Certificate
16638. Morgan County. [$98 estimated price]

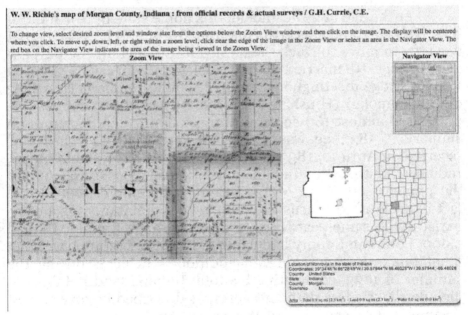

Figure 9 - Joshua Lindley land in Indiana

Summarizing these land purchases, they total 236.57
acres at an estimated total price of $294. An interesting note is
that the office of the President of the United States - Andrew
Jackson, signed all 3 land documents. Based upon Joshua's
relatively late marrying age of 27, he made sure he had the
resources to start a family prior to marriage, and executed his

plan to buy land immediately. A year later, his father began buying land adjacent to Joshua.

While most of Joshua's ancestors had focused on land acquisition followed by farming and a trade, Joshua pursued a different passion. Joshua was a pioneer in establishing the fruit growing industry in both Indiana and North Carolina. He described himself as a Pomologist, which is a fruit grower, on census records. He helped develop the foundations of fruit growing in the rapidly growing United States. He is credited with being the first nurseryman in Morgan County, Indiana as evidenced by the following account:

> In about 1830 the pioneer nursery of Morgan
> County was established at Monrovia by the late
> Joshua Lindley of North Carolina. For intelligence
> and enterprise among pioneer nurserymen of his
> day Mr. L stood in the front rank. He continued in
> the business at Monrovia until about 1843 when
> on account of climatic conditions he returned to
> his native State where he lived until a ripe old
> age...Mr. Lindley, while a resident of Indiana, was
> especially active in securing and testing new and
> promising varieties of fruits. The pear was a great
> favorite of his and he was beyond doubt the first to
> fruit the Bartlett within the borders of the State. Of
> this fact the Indiana Farmer for August 1840 page
> 3 bears me witness where the testing of the first
> specimen grown on his place is made a matter of
> record (Flick).

Joshua spent his time in Indiana growing, perfecting, and promoting fruit trees. He attended the first meeting of the Indiana Horticulture Society in August of 1840, as reported by W.H. Ragan:

> Of those who participated in this early meeting my
> parents often spoke in their later life. Indeed it was
> an epoch event in their otherwise quiet lives and

the theme was so fascinating for them and was so
frequently reiterated in the hearing of us children
that I almost feel as though I had really been there
and that I am now relating this as an original story. I have already said that James Blake was
chairman of this first meeting and that H.P. Co-
burn father of General John acted as secretary and
besides these Aaron Aldridge, Martin Williams,
Benjamin Morris, Cyrus R. Overman, James Siger-
son, Joshua Lindley and many others were present
and contributors to the exhibition. No prizes were
offered at this exhibition but many fine and rare
specimens of fruits bedecked the tables. Joshua
Lindley exhibited the first specimen grown in the
State of the justly celebrated Williams Bon Chre-
tien Bartlett pear. It was too precious to sample
but my parents were permitted to handle it and
sniff its fragrant perfume which they likened unto
that of a well ripened muskmelon. At the close of
the exhibition it was presented to the editor of the
Indiana Farmer who later had the following to say
of it: "It became perfectly mellow in a few days,
was very juicy and of excellent flavor and we can
recommend it as one of the best varieties of pears."
From a historical standpoint, this item is one of
much interest since from that day to this the Bartlett, all things considered, has been our most
popular and valuable pear (W. Ragan).

A friend, Robert Ragan, an early nurseryman in Ohio,
wrote a short biography of Joshua's time in Indiana in 1855. It
gives us a slightly different and more personal view as to why
the family returned to North Carolina:

Joshua Lindley moved from Chatham County,
North Carolina, and settled in Morgan County, Indiana, in or near the year 1831. Mr. Lindley was
tall, fair skinned, with brown hair and blue eyes,

full of urbanity, and free to converse, took great
delight in reading Pomological and Horticultural
works, and imparted information freely to his numerous friends. He started a small nursery near
Monrovia, where he used great exertion to bring
together all of the fine varieties of apples, peaches,
plums, cherries and pears, with the grape and all
the garden fruits. He read Van Mons's Theory [fur-
ther explained with J. Van Lindley's life below]
with a zeal, and the new pears with him were a real
hobby. He continued at Monrovia for ten years,
cultivating and disseminating largely all of the fine
fruits that would succeed well in his climate; at
length the rigors of northern climate made inroads
on his tender charges, among which was the health
of a young and beautiful wife, who had been reared
in the mild and sunny clime of the South. For the
sake of this greatest of all earthly blessings, in the
fall of 1841, he removed to Chatham County, North
Carolina, where he resumed his former occupation. Fourteen years have elapsed, and we now
find Joshua as the proprietor of the Pomological
Gardens and Nurseries at New Garden, Guilford
County, North Carolina, and also a Vice President
of the American Pomological Society (R. Ragan).

Joshua also attended the third meeting of the Society in
Indiana in 1842, despite the fact that he had recently moved
back to North Carolina. This demonstrated his commitment to
his profession, since the trip must have taken several weeks to
travel in each direction. He is also credited with being the first
nurseryman in North Carolina.

Joshua and Judith Henley had a total of 7 children together. Five, including John Van Mons Lindley, were born in
Monrovia, Indiana. The first of these children died after living
for only 3 months. The remaining 4 children and their parents
were granted a certificate by White Lick MM in Indiana on
December 15, 1841 to return to Spring MM in Chatham County,

NC where they were received on February 26, 1842 (Hinshaw 449). Upon their return, they settled once again in Chatham County. The couple's final two children were born in Chatham County over the next three years. Then, on Sept. 05, 1847, one day before her 35th birthday, Joshua's wife (J. Van Lindley's mother) Judith died.

Joshua's return to Chatham County, North Carolina was preceded on July 12, 1841 by the purchase of 3.75 acres from his Aunt Mary Lindley Braxton's son William. The family then left Indiana in December and arrived at their new home in early 1842. Joshua bought the land for $30 and then followed it up with the purchase of 307 acres for $775 from another cousin, Thomas Lindley, in 1845. Although he had paid $1.25 per acre for his Indiana land, the land in North Carolina was costing him $2.50 per acre. He sold most of his land back to Thomas Lindley in 1848 and 1849 for about the same amount.

The return of Joshua to North Carolina marked the beginning of the nursery business in the state. In the book Greensboro, 1808-1904, Facts, Figures, Traditions, and Reminiscences, Joshua is described as:

> "...the first man in the State to establish the growing of nursery stock for general sale, and leading authority upon all matters pertaining to the growing of fruits or cultivation of fruit trees." (Albright 90)

Joshua and his six children are listed in the 1850 U.S. Federal Census as living in Upper Regiment, Chatham, North Carolina. Joshua is listed as 46 years old and a Pomologist with his land valued at $900. J. Van is 13 and his older brother Albert is 19 years old. Albert's occupation is listed as a farmer. His cousin, Thomas P. Lindley, also lists "Pomologist" as his profession in the same census, so the two could have been working together, although there was nothing found to substantiate this conjecture (United States Government).

Figure 10 - Joshua and Mary K. Lindley

On October 2, 1851 Joshua married Mary K. Owen. This marriage must have introduced some interesting relationship challenges within the family because Mary was 16 at the time of their marriage. By comparison, Joshua's children were: Albert, 20, who was older than his new mother, Phoebe Jane, 16, who about the same age as Mary K., and J. Van, 14, who was only two years younger. It also probably caused a problem within the Spring MM Quaker fold because Joshua was condemned for breach of order, the only recorded censure found for him.

Joshua's oldest daughter Phoebe Jane died a year later in August of 1852 and the entire family relocated to Guilford County, NC within two months. On October 30, 1852, Joshua, Mary and his 5 remaining children were granted a certificate by the Spring MM to move to New Garden MM in Guilford, NC. They were received by their new congregation on November 24, 1852 (Hinshaw 557).

The move to Greensboro had everything to do with business potential. The entire Piedmont Area of North Carolina had been plagued with transportation problems since the first settlers arrived. This area of North Carolina did not have deep-water rivers or canals for moving goods. Canals were built in the northeastern United States during the first half of the 19th Century, as well as being supplemented by natural waterways that provided business advantages to the northern states. Central North Carolina had limited road structures, poor road conditions, and the result was slow movement of goods. Until hard surface roads were created early in the twentieth century, the roads were mostly impassable from November to March. For perishable farm products, this only left a local market to serve.

These issues were well recognized within North Carolina. Beginning as early as 1828, meetings began to be held to discuss solutions. At a meeting held on August 1, 1828 in Chatham County 200 interested citizens from Chatham, Guilford, Orange, and Randolph counties attended. They created a group that went forward to the State of North Carolina and proposed a railroad from the seaport to the state capital and then on to the western extremity of the state. Joshua Lindley's uncle, also named Joshua, attended this meeting as a representative from Chatham County. The North Carolina Railroad was finally built in the early 1850's:

> Appropriately, ceremonies marking the beginning
> and end of construction on the North Carolina
> Railroad took place in Greensboro or its environs.
> At the first railroad meeting in Greensboro, July 4,
> [in the late 1840's] Mr. Joshua Lindley came up
> from Chatham County bringing a crate of the first
> ripe peaches. The Guilford County seat was posi-
> tioned near the midpoint of the 223-mile arch that
> the road followed across the state from Charlotte
> to Goldsboro. The early annual meetings of the
> stockholders were held in the Gate City. And, most
> importantly, Greensboro was the home of John
> Motley Morehead, former governor (1841–1845)
> and "in large measure the road's founding father,"
> according to railroad historian Allen W. Trelease

(North Carolina Highway Historical Marker
Program, marker J-102).

The formal groundbreaking took place on Friday, July 11,
1851, following the annual stockholders meeting. Thousands
attended and the crowd was judged by the local paper to be the
largest in the town's history. Morehead spoke, voicing his pride
in the project. Calvin Graves of Caswell County, who had sacri-
ficed his political career by casting the deciding vote in favor of
the railroad, had the honor of turning the first spade of soil.
Those assembled filled a chest that served as a time capsule.
Five years later, the two track-laying crews met at "Hilltop"
midway between Jamestown and Greensboro. David F. Caldwell
of Greensboro, legislator and railroad backer, drove the final
spike. The Greensborough Patriot (The Greensborough Patriot)
of February 1, 1856, headlined "Finished!!" and the Greensboro
Times of January 21, 1856, "The Road Completed!"(Greensboro
Times).

Along with other progressive leaders, Joshua Lindley had
looked at the new railroad, which did not come through where
he lived in Chatham County, and decided to move to a location
close to one of the new train stations. This decision had clear
strategic advantages, but the main beneficiary of his foresight,
as we shall see later, was his son J. Van Lindley. By the time the
railroad was completed in 1856, Joshua was well placed to use
the new system to extend the reach of his fruit bearing trees and
fruit products. He described his rationale and vision for moving
in the introduction to his 1857 catalog:

> These nurseries are now being removed and locat-
> ed in view of the North Carolina Central Railroad
> at (or in the vicinity of) New Garden, Guilford
> County, N.C., five miles West of Greensborough.
> The proprietor has been induced to remove his
> nurseries to a site on this giant thoroughfare, un-
> der an impression that when it is finished, and the
> other Railroads, River improvements, and Plank
> roads that are going on in our State, it will give

great and prompt facility to send packages of trees to every man's trading town or depot in the State, or any of the Southern or Western States (J. Lindley, Catalogue of Fruit Trees (From 1857 to 1860)).

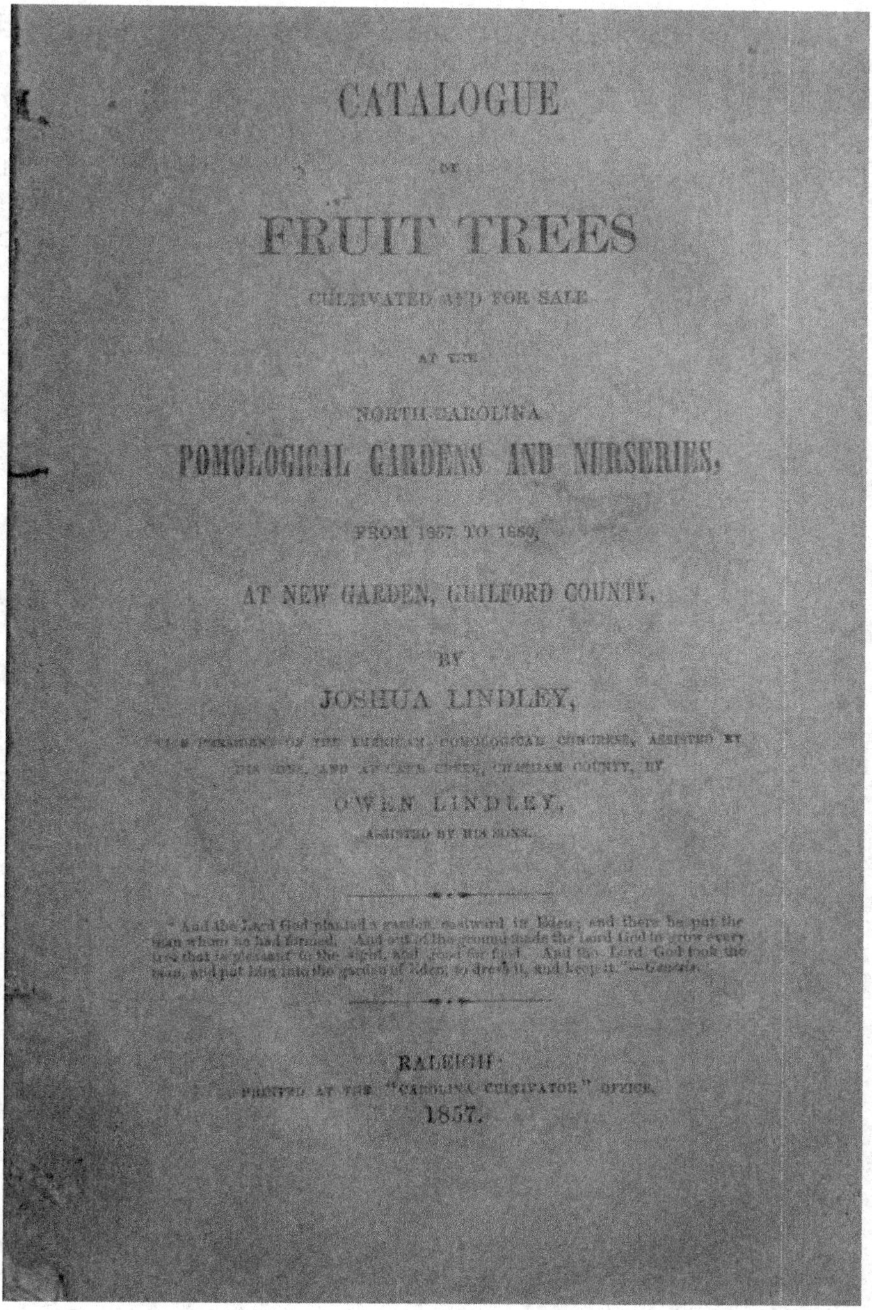

CATALOGUE

OF

FRUIT TREES

CULTIVATED AND FOR SALE

AT THE

NORTH-CAROLINA

POMOLOGICAL GARDENS AND NURSERIES,

FROM 1857 TO 1858,

AT NEW GARDEN, GUILFORD COUNTY,

BY

JOSHUA LINDLEY,

VICE PRESIDENT OF THE AMERICAN POMOLOGICAL CONGRESS, ASSISTED BY HIS SONS, AND AT CANE CREEK, CHATHAM COUNTY, BY

OWEN LINDLEY,

ASSISTED BY HIS SONS.

"And the Lord God planted a garden eastward in Eden; and there he put the man whom he had formed. And out of the ground made the Lord God to grow every tree that is pleasant to the sight, and good for food. And the Lord God took the man, and put him into the garden of Eden, to dress it, and keep it."—*Genesis.*

RALEIGH:

PRINTED AT THE "CAROLINA CULTIVATOR" OFFICE.

1857.

Figure 11 - Joshua Lindley Catalog of Fruit Trees

In the same catalog, Joshua mentions that it is the fourth catalog. The oldest available catalogs found are the 1853-56 (J. Lindley, Catalogue of fruit trees, cultivated and for sale at the North-Carolina Pomological Garden and Nurseries from 1853 to 1856) and 1857-60 catalogs, both of which are preserved in the North Carolina Collection at the UNC-Chapel Hill Library. They each contain a list of the fruit trees and plants available for purchase, as shown in this summary of the 1853-56 catalog:

Apples - 10 cents each, pages 5-7, 160 varieties

Peaches - 10 cents each, pages 8-9, 103 varieties

Pears - 50 cents each, 75 cents to $1.00 for the largest size, pages 10-11, 112 varieties

Plums - 25 cents, extra large trees higher, pages 12-13

Cherries - 25 cents, extra large trees higher, page 14, 51 varieties

Apricots - 25 cents, page 15, 18 varieties

Nectarines - 25 cents, page 15, 15 varieties

Grapes - 25 cents, page 16, 18 varieties

Strawberries - 25-50 cents per dozen, $1-2 per 100 according to kinds, page 16, 9 varieties

Raspberries - 10 cents a plant, 25 cents per half dozen, page 17, 5 varieties

Quinces - 4 varieties, page 17

Currants - 3 varieties, page 17

Figs - 25 cents, 5 varieties, page 17

Directions for planting, page 18

The new home for the Lindley family also placed them near the 15-year-old New Garden Boarding School, the precursor to Guilford College. Joshua had not received the benefit of an education, but he was able to give three of his children -

Albert, Caroline and J. Van - a chance to attend school. According to a review of school records, Albert and Caroline were able to attend for a few years and J. Van was only able to attend for one semester. At that time, most of the residents of Guilford County were subsistence farmers, including Joshua. Joshua had to send his children to Guilford Boarding School on credit. He had a running tab with the school that was eventually converted to a bond representing the debt he owed them. The school's records show that he carried forward a balance of $29.65 after Caroline's first semester, $49.86 after the second, $112.88 after the third (April 12, 1855), and then $158.05 was settled by bond after the fourth semester. A year later, he carried forward $111.53 for 2 more semesters for Caroline. Finally, he added $58.07 for one semester for John, less $10.20 for 6 weeks of "lost time." The final entry was for a second bond of $159.40 of debt that Joshua owed the school (Guilford College). No evidence was found that he paid off the debt, which, unfortunately for the school, was not unusual in their early years.

When Joshua moved to Guilford County, he may have already owned 185 acres that he bought from John H. Iddings and James Gordon on August 10, 1851. There is no record of him buying or either of the two parties selling land based upon a review of the county records. However, he was able to borrow successfully against that land many times, so it can be assumed that he did own the land. Joshua borrowed repeatedly for the remaining 30 years of his life. He generally borrowed during the winter months of November to February, always borrowing against the 185-acre tract of land, from 1852 through 1859. There were no transactions listed again until 1871. The Civil War began in 1861 and continued until April of 1865. The South, including Guilford County, was devastated. According to an account by J. Van Lindley, his father owed $5,000 following the Civil War (Baker).

Joshua and J. Van Lindley joined forces when J. Van returned from war. The next land transaction by Joshua was a purchase of 164 acres for $800 in 1871. Beginning in 1874, he began borrowing again during the winter months, borrowing first $500 in 1874 and then $250 in 1875. In December of 1876 he purchased another 160 acres, this time paying $2,000 for land owned by George Lincoln, but borrowing the whole amount owed from George Lincoln. He repeatedly borrowed against this land until he owed the Guilford Building and Loan Association (GBLA) $2,250, then $1,500 a year later, plus 2nd and 3rd mortgages to two suppliers. In January of 1879, he got a loan from the GBLA secured by:

> "two mules, one two horse wagon, iron axle, one
> old buggy, one gray mare, four head of cattle, one
> milk cow and three other cattle, one spring wagon,
> one double set wagon harness, one set buggy har-
> ness, one sulky and..." [other personal property]
> (Guilford County Register of Deeds) .

Joshua's total land holdings equaled about 550 acres at their height and, as mentioned, they were usually heavily mortgaged. Joshua was not able to enjoy the outstanding wealth creation opportunities available to his ancestors. However, he developed a widely known and well-deserved reputation for understanding the trade of fruit growing. He was one of the founders of the American Pomological Society in 1848, an organization that is still vibrant over 160 years later and is the oldest fruit organization in North America. Finally, he gave J. Van Lindley an excellent education in the trade, positioning J. Van Lindley along the railroad tracks so that the fruit tree business could flourish to a level never possible during Joshua's life.

The exact date of Joshua's death has not been found in any available records. He signed his will on June 29, 1880 and the probate was on June 6, 1881, so the date of his death should have been sometime between these two dates.

Joshua Lindley's Will

> Last will and testament: As I am able to judge
> rightly and believe in my health failing somewhat I
> think it best to arrange my affairs in writing suita-

ble to my wants and desires to this end I bequeath the following property [unreadable] the Lincoln Place now deeded to me bought of George Lincoln the place being situated in Morehead Township Guilford County North Carolina and adjoining the following parties to with on the west by James Joyce on the north by Yancey Ballinger and Alford Engold on the East by John Van Lindley on the south by Mrs. Emily Armfield containing about 170 acres this place as above described I give or bequeath to my son Jesse Clarkson Lindley as I consider I am due him that for conducting and managing my part of the business

And the home place I give or bequeath to my youngest child Samuel Passmore Lindley this place is situated in Friendship Township Guilford County North Carolina and adjoining the following persons on the west by John Van Lindley and William Walker on the north by John Van Lindley and Milton Stanley and on the east by William Wormack and Emsley H. Schuler on the South by John Walker and Henry Rush and it is understood that myself and my wife Mary K. Lindley are to have a life time right to the home place and then go to my son as before said Samuel Lindley according to contract made between myself and my son Jesse Clarkson Lindley dated January 1, 1880 in which it is agreed on by distinctly and fully understood and which I reassert in this last will and testament that he is owner of one half of the entire nursery stock of the nurseries known as New Garden Nurseries and that he is owner of one half of all personal property and I further in this writing make it explicitly understood that I give him one half interior of the whole nurseries and one half of personal property as named in contract

And I in this my last will and testament give or bequeath to my son Charles Sumner Lindley the other half of my half interest of the entire nurseries and the other half of my half of the personal property

To my son Albert G. Lindley I bequeath the sum of five dollars to my son John Van Lindley I bequeath the sum of five dollars to my son William Downing Lindley I bequeath the sum of $25 to my daughters Callie Victoria and Sophronia P. Lindley I bequeath the sum of $10 each. All of the above to be paid in one year after my decease. And for carrying out and accomplishment of these bequeaths and desires of this my last will and testament I appoint my son Jesse Clarkston Lindley as executor of my affairs without here requiring him to give bond having confidence in his honesty integrity and ability and I give him full power and authority to arrange and settle all debts against me or the firm as he knows and thinks best and giving him full power to collect any and all claims due me or firm and to settle all my affairs in every way justly and to the best advantage

And in witness whereof I offer my hand and signature of this date June 29, A.D. 1880

Signed

Joshua Lindley

We the undersigned at the request and in the presence of Joshua Lindley witness the execution of this foregoing paper writing which he declares to be his last will and testament and in the presence of each other have here unto subscribed our names as witnesses thereto

William Walker
Williamson M. Edwards
WJ Edmundson

Summary of the terms of the will

Jesse Clarkson [executor]

inherits 170 acres in Morehead Township

Samuel Passmore

inherits the home place situated in Friendship Township and one half of the entire nursery stock, personal property, and interior of New Garden Nurseries

Charles Sumner

inherits the other half interest in and personal property of New Garden Nurseries

Joshua and wife Mary K

inherit a lifetime right to the home place

Other Sons:

Albert G. - $5
John Van - $5
William Downing - $25

Daughters:

Callie (Queen) Victoria - $10
Sophronia P. - $10
Caroline - not mentioned
Emma - not mentioned
Judith - not mentioned
Roxia - not mentioned

The will was processed in probate court on June 6, 1881 by J.C. [Jesse Clarkson] Lindley. In the Application for Letters Testamentary document, which Jesse filed, the combined real and personal estate was estimated to be worth $5,000. On the same date J.C. Lindley agreed, under the Executor's Oath, to pay the debts and then the legacies to fulfill his duties as executor. The original will and executor documents are on file in the

North Carolina State Archives in Raleigh, NC (N.C. State Archives).

Due to Joshua's debts, his land was forced to be sold at auction by George Lincoln. Two hundred acres were sold for a total of $1,500 on November 6, 1882. Joshua's sons Jesse Clarkson Lindley and Samuel Passmore Lindley were able to continue operating as J.C. Lindley & Bro until 1890 when J. Van Lindley was made trustee to cultivate their remaining trees, pay their debts, and collect amounts due to them.

1838 - 1861: Birth to Adult

Birth to Civil War

John Van Mons Lindley (J. Van Lindley) was born on November 5, 1838 in the town of Monrovia in Morgan County, Indiana. As we already know from studying his father's life, Joshua was an ardent Pomologist. Joshua's interest was so keen that he read everything he could on the subject and was recognized as an expert in Indiana, North Carolina, and at the national meetings, which he attended of the American Pomological Society. Joshua's passion, knowledge and experience were passed on to J. Van early in life. In fact, it started when J. Van was named by his father for two individuals:

> John Lindley, the originator of the famous Chelsea Flower Show, who was possibly a distant relative, but more importantly he was the primary scholarly authority on fruit plants and the field of Botany. Joshua spent a great deal of time studying his books, such as the <u>Encyclopedia of Plants</u> or <u>An Introduction to the Natural System of Botany</u>.

> Jean-Baptiste Van Mons, who carried out the first recorded selective breeding of the European Pear through cycles of seed propagation. He produced 40 superior varieties over a 60-year period, readily sharing his observations and plants, and developing effective methods for exporting cuttings and seedlings, including to the United States.

It is fitting that these two namesakes were combined and placed on this particular man - John Van Mons Lindley - because most of his life was devoted to growing all types of plants, flowers, and shrubs; but always with the love of fruit trees being his primary focus.

J. Van was barely 3 years old in 1841 when his family returned to Chatham County, North Carolina where his parents had been born and raised (the area became Alamance County in 1849). He lived there with his parents for 5 years until his mother's death. When his family moved to New Garden, his older brother Albert G. and younger sister Caroline were able to attend New Garden Boarding School for several years. J. Van was only able to attend for one semester. The exact reason for this is not known, but is speculated about in this biographical sketch:

> "Close application to his occupations left him little
> opportunity for study and one year at the New
> Garden School completed the limited college
> course for which he had leisure outside of the les-
> sons in pomology and horticulture learned in farm
> and garden. Toward these pursuits both natural
> and inherited tendency led him and he threw him-
> self into them with all the ardor and earnestness
> which have been his characteristics through life"
> (Ashe, Weeks and Van Noppen).

The reason for J. Van's short education may also have had to do with awkward family dynamics and economics. Joshua's young wife was only 6 years older than Caroline, which may have necessitated prioritizing getting Caroline out of the home. Meanwhile, Joshua may have needed J. Van to help in the fields since, based upon his record of payment to the school, Joshua was not able to afford the tuition for three children. A review of the manual ledgers at New Garden Boarding School reveal that Joshua ran up a tuition bill, which went unpaid, was then carried forward, and eventually converted into a bond. He owed $101.06 prior to May, 1855, then $160.05 by November 1, 1855, which was "Settled by Bond." On August 5th, 1857 he "Settled by

Bond" again for $159.40 after only one session for J. Van (Guilford College).

J. Van continued to live at home through his 21st birthday. On July 14, 1860 the U.S. Census records him as being 21 and living with his father. Joshua is listed as an "Agriculturist" with a land value of $3,000 and a personal value of $300. Caroline had followed the example of her stepmother and married a man 10 years her elder when she was 18 years old. Sometime after this date, J. Van set off alone to see the world and decide how and where to make his fortune. Family tradition has it that he travelled and worked in both Texas and Missouri during this time. J. Van had some distant relatives in Texas whom he may have visited, but there is no record for this period in his life, only references. However, as we shall soon see, there are records that he was living and working with his older brother Albert in Missouri, so he went to visit him. It was there that the drumbeat of the Civil War reached his ears as he and his brother worked the land on the farm of a fellow Quaker from Pennsylvania.

1862 - 1865: Civil War Soldier

The advent of the American Civil War or War Between the States posed an interesting dilemma for Quakers on two fronts. First, the Quaker "Declaration of Pacifism" was made in 1660, in the early days of the religion, to Charles II:

> "We utterly deny all outward wars and strife, and fighting with outward weapons, for any end, or under any pretense whatever; this is our testimony to the whole world. The Spirit of Christ by which we are guided is not changeable, so as once to command us from a thing as evil, and again to move unto it; and we certainly know, and testify to the world, that the Spirit of Christ, which leads us into all truth, will never move us to fight and war against any man with outward weapons, neither

for the kingdom of Christ, nor for the kingdoms of
this world" (Tokyo Monthly Meeting).

While this Quaker belief and tradition was strong in prin-
ciple, in practice it was not universally adopted. As previously
discussed, a few of J. Van Lindley's relatives had participated in
armed conflicts during the Revolutionary War time period.

The second issue had to do with slavery. The Quakers
took a stand against slavery beginning in the late 17th Century
as described in this account:

"The early position of the Society of Friends
(Quakers) as to slavery, for a time was like that of
other religious groups of the day, they accepted it.
The Negro slaves were generally well treated by
the early Friends, and leaders like George Fox and
William Penn and others considered the blacks to
be human beings. They also pressed for slaves to
be set free after a term of service. In 1688, Ger-
mantown Pennsylvania Friends were concerned
enough about slavery to prepare a protest 'against
the traffic in the bodies of men, and against han-
dling men like cattle,' which was forwarded to the
Quarterly Meeting and Yearly Meeting. This is be-
lieved to be the first official protest against slavery
of any religious body in America. This protest
against slavery was taken up by Benjamin Lay and
John Woolman who visited widely among Friends
sharing their message that the Quakers should
recognize the evils of slavery and free their slaves.
The Quakers responded to this message of concern
and love, and before the end of the 18th century no
slaves were held by Friends in America" (Savage).

The impact of not owning slaves, and being against slavery was felt directly and personally by Quakers who lived in
central North Carolina. Working the land with slave labor was
much more profitable for large landowners than trying to work

it without slave labor. In reality, few families had more than 10 slaves, but the families with large plantations dictated the social values. Families without slaves were looked down upon. The slave-owning families hated groups that helped runaway slaves, like the New Garden MM.

As the Quakers migrated to Indiana, specifically to escape these attitudes and practices, they smuggled escaped slaves with them. Although there is no direct evidence that J. Van was involved or sympathetic with any of these practices, he was a stalwart member of the community that engaged in these activities.

The outbreak of the Civil War found J. Van living with his older brother Albert in Missouri, working for an older Quaker who moved to Indiana from Pennsylvania. They each had to decide whether or not to participate and, if so, on which side. They were from the South, lived in the Northern region of a border state, were declared pacifists, but came from a group dedicated to ending slavery.

J. Van's decision was described in a biographical sketch written about him:

> "Soon after arriving at manhood the War Between the States broke out and Lincoln's call for troops forced every Southern man to make decision as to the side with which his sympathies lay. Mr. Lindley chose to espouse the Northern cause and although of Quaker parentage both father and mother being members of the Society of Friends he fought bravely for three years as a private in the regular cavalry of Missouri in the Federal army" (Ashe, Weeks and Van Noppen).

J. Van and Albert Lindley enlisted on April 1, 1862 and were mustered in on April 3, 1865 (Missouri Secretary of State). There is very little information available about J. Van Lindley's direct participation in the conflict, but there is a lot known about the Missouri State Militia, battles within the state, and how the State of Missouri sat in the cross hairs of the Civil War conflict.

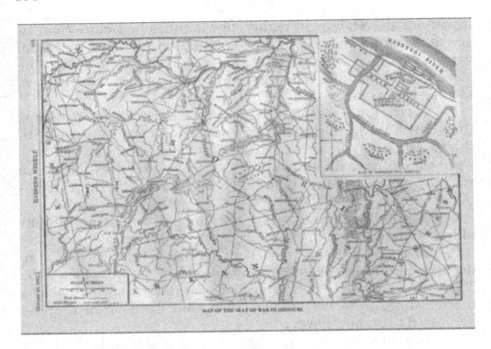

Figure 12 - The Civil War in Southwest Missouri

Beginning in the 1850's, the Missouri-Kansas border had been the dividing line for a bloody struggle over the question of slavery in Kansas. Between 1854 and 1859 pro- and anti-slavery forces ambushed and raided each other in an attempt to control the future of Kansas. This fighting prepared Missourians for the type of Civil War they would encounter within the country's great struggle.

By 1860 Missouri was a state in change. In the ten years before the war the original Southern settlers of the state discovered themselves sharing the land with a large contingent of German immigrants. These newcomers were staunchly anti-slavery. As the country lurched toward war in 1861, newly elected Governor Claiborne F. Jackson led the pro-slavery forces in Missouri. Leading the anti-slavery group were Congressman Francis P. Blair and General Nathaniel Lyon.

In 1861 General Lyon headed up the anti-slavery Federal Troop as they fought Governor Jackson's State Militia, known as The Missouri State Guard, from May until November. Lyon pursued an aggressive stance and pushed the confederate lean-ing Missouri Militia south and west from St. Louis until they ended up in Arkansas. Fighting went back and forth across Missouri's southern border until General Lyon was killed on August 10, but not before rendering the confederates incapable of further movements until the following spring (Missouri's Civil War Heritage Foundation).

Confederate General Sterling Price was openly support-ing guerrilla activity in Missouri by the spring of 1862 and on March 13, in retaliation, the Union head of the Department of the Missouri, General Henry Halleck, issued orders stating that such activity was "contrary to the laws of war" and directed that such combatants "will be hung as robbers and murderers." The next month, Confederate President Jefferson Davis legitimized guerrilla warfare by authorizing bands of "partisan rangers" to be formed to operate behind Federal lines. As the primary force to confront such activity in Missouri, the Missouri State Militia (which by that time was on the federal, anti-slavery side) hierar-chy shortly afterwards issued a controversial order declaring the partisans to be "robbers and assassins" and directing that they "be shot down on the spot." The order further offered the parti-sans an out, stating that they would be spared should they surrender to Federal authorities and take an oath of allegiance and be placed on parole. Some militia commanders were after-wards accused of atrocities in carrying out the counter-guerrilla tactics, including conducting drum-head court martial, or sometimes not court martial at all and summarily executing suspected guerrillas or Southerners who had violated their paroles (Nichols, 2004). There were also several examples of the execution of prisoners in retaliation for the deaths of Un-ion/militia soldiers or citizens.

After enlisting in the Missouri State Militia in the spring of 1862, J. Van was assigned to "Company D" and put to work as a saddler and buffalo hunter. Albert was a Sergeant. For exactly three years, the two served together protecting the state of Missouri.

When the two brothers began training with the Missouri State Militia, the warming weather also brought out increased guerrilla activity. Confederate recruiters infiltrated the state and began organizing new commands to be sent south. This accelerated the learning curve for the new militia cavalry (Nichols). Despite setbacks and a surge in Confederate activity even north of the Missouri River, the Missouri Militia Cavalry proved to be an effective offensive force in confronting guerrillas, recruiters, and raiders within the state during the summer of 1862. By autumn the Confederate recruiters had been driven from the state. Although guerrilla activity would remain a constant nuisance in much of the state, and raids would continue south of the Missouri River, the militia cavalry established Federal control of Missouri throughout the remainder of the war. An unusual aspect of the militia cavalry compared to conventional cavalry was the frequent integration of light artillery into regimental or battalion level actions. The additional firepower was often effective against guerrillas or raiders with no artillery of their own (Nichols) (United States War Department).

There was considerable controversy and intrigue surrounding the actions, officers and men of the Missouri State Militia Cavalry. Several officers were at times charged with inefficiency or worse during operations, particularly during Sterling Price's 1864 Raid. General Alfred Pleasonton relieved General Egbert Brown, the commanding general that J. Van's and Albert's regiment reported to, and John McNeil for "failure to obey an order to attack" (Warner). Also relieved by Pleasonton in the same action was Colonel James McFerran of the 1st Missouri State Militia Cavalry "whose regiment was straggling all over the country and he was neglecting to prevent it" (United States War Department). Colonel Henry S. Lipscomb of the 11th Missouri State Militia Cavalry was relieved for not pursuing Joseph C. Porter more vigorously during the summer of 1862 (Nichols) (United States War Department) (Mudd) and the regiment was consolidated with the 2nd.

In contrast to these controversies, Governor Hamilton R. Gamble, praised the Missouri State Militia as being "very efficient." In speaking of the Missouri State Militia, General John M. Schofield claimed that "these troops will compare favorably with any volunteer troops I have seen," specifically complimenting the Missouri State Militia in regard to drill, discipline and efficiency. Schofield subsequently became General-in-Chief of the United States Army after the war (United States Record and Pension Office) (Ross).

The Missouri State Militia was primarily comprised of cavalry units, like the 4th Regiment, and they participated in most of the significant engagements in the state of Missouri from 1862 to 1864. Since there are no direct references to Company D having served in specific conflicts, reviewing a significant summary of their service record helps to get an understanding of the types of encounters and scope of their activity.

In the summary that follows, note that:

First, except for a brief trip into Arkansas in October of 1862, the unit stayed within the southwest quadrant of Missouri.

Second, they reported to Brigadier General Egbert B. Brown for most of this time, until he was relieved in 1864.

Third, they spent most of their time suppressing Confederate guerrillas and opposing raids from Arkansas and the Indian Territory.

Fourth, their main Confederate enemy leaders were General Sterling Price, Brigadier General John Sappington Marmaduke, Colonel John Trousdale Coffee, Colonel Joseph O. Shelby and Capt. William Clarke Quantrill (who led a group of ruffians that included the notorious James brothers: Jesse and Frank) (Wikipedia).

4th Regiment Missouri State Militia Calvary Service Summary

Organized at St. Joseph, Mo., January 28 to May 14, 1862.

Ordered to Kansas City, Mo., May, 1862, and duty fitting out until August , 1862.

Skirmish on Little Blue River, June 2, 1862.

Ordered to Southwest Missouri August, 1862, attached to District of Southwest Missouri, Dept. of Missouri, to December, 1862, and reported to General Egbert B. Brown.

Pursuit of Colonel Coffee, August 8-September 1, 1862.

Between Stockton and Humansville and near Stockton August 12, 1862.

Duty at Mt. Vernon till September 30, 1862.

Joined Totten's Division, Army of the Frontier, at Oxford Bend, near Fayetteville, Ark., October 27-28, 1862.

Expedition from Greenfield into Jasper and Barton Counties November 24-26, 1862.

District of Central Missouri, Dept. of Missouri, December, 1862 to July, 1863.

Operations against General Marmaduke in Missouri, December 31, 1862-January 25, 1863.

Defense of Springfield, Mo., January 8, 1863.

Duty in central Missouri and guarding the Missouri Pacific Railroad, with Headquarters at LaMine Bridge, Jefferson City, Tipton, Sedalia and Warrensburg, Mo. until October, 1864.

Operations about Princeton, Mo. May 4, 1863.

Waverly, Mo. June 1 (Cos. "B" and "C"), 1863.

Sibley, Mo. June 23 (4 Cos.). Marshall, Mo. July 28. Saline County, Mo. July 30, 1863.

District of the Border, Dept. of Missouri, July, 1863 to January, 1864.

Operations against Captain Quantrell, August 20-28, 1863.

Operations against Colonel Shelby September 22-October 26. Tipton and Syracuse, Mo. October 10 (Cos. "A," "B," "E" and "F"), Booneville, Mo. October 11-12, 1863.

Merrill's Landing and Dug Ford, near Jonesborough, Mo. October 12, 1863.

Marshall, Arrow Rock, Blackwater, Mo. October 13, 1863.

District of Central Missouri, Dept. of Missouri, January, 1864 to July, 1865.

Operations about Warrensburg, Mo. February 22-24, 1864.

Scout from Sedalia to Blackwater, Mo. June 3-5 (Co. "E"), 1864.

Near Sedalia, Mo. and Marshall Road June 26 (Co. "E"), 1864.

Huntsville, Mo. July 16. Scout from Independence to Lafayette County August 7-8 (Detachment), 1864.

Operations in Lafayette and Saline Counties August 13-22 (Detachment), 1864.

Near Roeheport, Mo. August 28 (Detachment), 1864.

Howard County August 28 (Co. "E"), 1864.

Defense of Jefferson City, Mo. October 1, 1864.

Campaign against General Price October, 1864:

Moreau Bottoms, Mo. October 7.
California, Mo. October 9.
Booneville, Mo. October 9-12.
Little Blue River, October 21.

Independence, Mo., Big Blue River and State
Line October 22.
Engagement at the Marmiton, Mo. or battle
of Chariot October 25, Mine Creek, Mo.
Westport, Mo. October 23.
Little Osage River and Marias de. Cygnes,
Mo. October.

At Sedalia, Mo., November, 1864, to April, 1865.

Scout In Calloway County November 6-7, 1864
(Detachment moved to St. Louis April, 1865, and
most of Regiment mustered out April 18, 1865,
Balance mustered out July 8, 1865.

Killed and wounded:

Regiment lost during service 2 Officers and
34 Enlisted men killed and mortally wounded
and 2 Officers and 86 Enlisted men by disease
for a total of 124 dead (Dyer).

J. Van Lindley served his country for exactly 3 years and
mustered out on April 3, 1865. His brother Albert re-enlisted for
another 2 years. The Missouri State Militia were eligible for re-
enlistment and, unusual for militia, were eligible for Federal
pensions beginning in February, 1895 (Ross). J. Van Lindley
filed for and received his pension.

As evidenced by the regiment's service summary, they
were active and most likely moved frequently. Company D is not
specifically listed as participating directly in any campaign. It
may be that they were a support unit for the rest of their regiment's cavalry based upon J. Van's role as a "horse saddler and
buffalo hunter." During the war, buffalo hides were used by the
military (Botkin) and buffalo coats were popular (Fanny &
Vera).

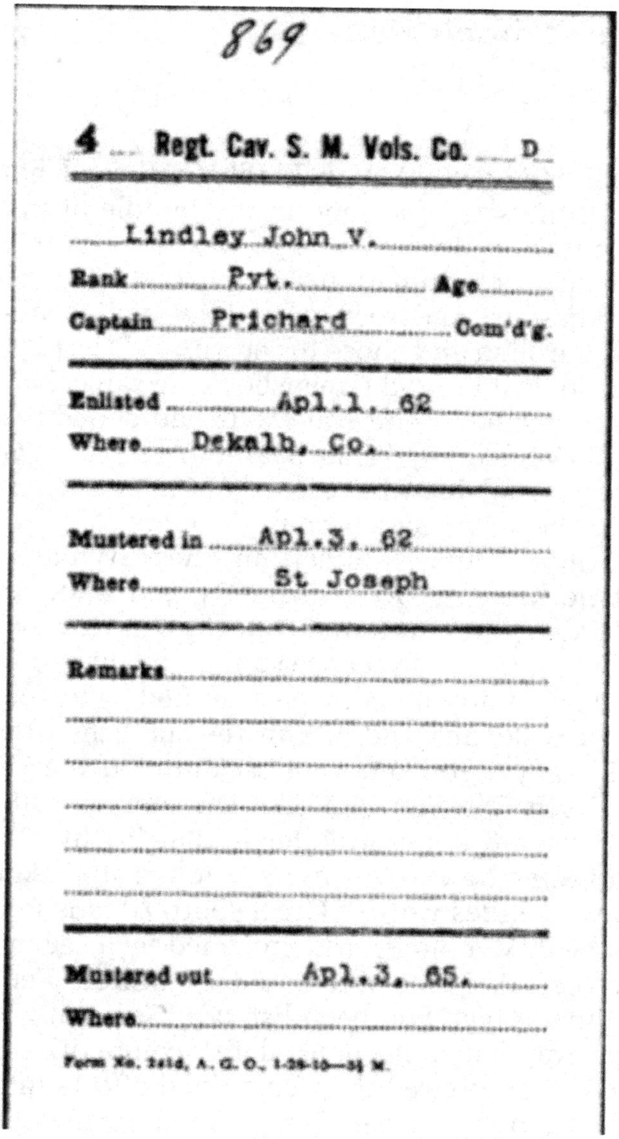

869

4 Regt. Cav. S. M. Vols. Co. D

Lindley John V.

Rank Pvt. Age

Captain Prichard Com'd'g.

Enlisted Apl. 1. 62

Where Dekalb, Co.

Mustered in Apl. 3. 62

Where St Joseph

Remarks

Mustered out Apl. 3. 65.

Where

Form No. 2414, A. G. O., 1-26-10—34 M.

Figure 13 - J. Van Lindley Civil War Record

(Missouri Secretary of State).

1866 - 1891: Pomologist

1866-1880

At the age of 26, J. Van Lindley returned home with a powder mark the size of a dime in the middle of his forehead. This small outward physical change was more than offset by a new confidence, determination and purpose. He had been to Texas and Missouri and seen what they had to offer, but he loved North Carolina and chose to return.

As he looked around Greensboro, he saw a beaten South. Confederacy President Jefferson Davis had ended his run from Richmond in Greensboro. While spared from battle, Greensboro had been busy supplying what turned out to be a losing cause. In the process, the town had become economically ruined. This included Joshua Lindley's nursery business. While Joshua had stated that he had $3,000 in property and $300 in personal assets in 1860, J. Van now found New Garden Nursery in debt to the extent of $5,000, an immense sum at the time.

The character of a man is determined by his performance under pressure. Joshua and J. Van re-established the business as Joshua Lindley & Son and went back into business in 1866. In Branson's North Carolina Business Directory for 1867-8 published by Branson & Jones in Raleigh, they list five Nurserymen in Guilford County, NC: Westbrook & Albright, Joshua Lindley, J.V. Lindsay - 5 miles west of Greensboro [this is a misspelling and should be J. V. Lindley, as confirmed by a second listing of Nurserymen], C.P. Mendenhall and J. Milton Fentress. The same five Nurserymen had been listed in Branson's 1860 directory, so the war had not changed the competitive landscape. Joshua and J. Van poured their combined efforts into the business and it began to prosper. Ten years later they found themselves debt free. J. Van's character, fired by the blaze of battle, challenged by a mountain of economic debt, and tested during the darkest of Southern times, was just beginning to come through.

The 1870 census came soon after his marriage to Mary Coffin on May 25, the daughter of a well-known Quaker family from New Garden Monthly Meeting. J. Van and Mary were listed as living next door to his father Joshua. They had a property value of $1,000 and a personal estate of $200 (United States Government 1870). Mary's cousins Levi Coffin (cousin to her father Nathan) and Addison Coffin had been heavily involved in the Underground Railroad. Levi moved to Indiana in 1826 with his young family. Addison followed him in 1845, first marrying and then moving. From Indiana, both participated in the Underground Railroad and Levi became known as the "President of the Underground Railroad" although there was no such title and his contribution was equaled by others in more eastern states. What is well documented is that the Quaker religion and New Garden Monthly Meeting in particular were consistently involved in promoting the emancipation of slaves, even prior to the Revolutionary War. While many slaves escaped from border states, few were able to leave from deeper in the South, with the exception of the New Garden area outside of Greensboro, NC.

Mary Coffin did not live long after they married. She died less than a year later on April 12, 1871 and the cause of her death is not known. It was possibly related to a pregnancy or childbirth, but there is no available evidence. At 33 years old, J. Van had already seen the death of his mother, the worst war on American soil, the near bankruptcy of his father, the economic malaise of the South following the war and now the death of his young wife. Many men would have crumbled under this onslaught of setbacks.

Mary's death, though tragic, was not unusual. The lack of modern medical care and sanitary practices routinely led to shortened lives. In one extreme example, a distant Indiana relative named James Lindley (who was born April 18, 1813) lived until he was 43 years old. His wife lived until she was 56. Six of their nine children were dead before the age of twenty-five. Accepting the early death of loved ones was a reality of nineteenth century life in America.

As mentioned by his biographer, George Grimsley, J. Van continued his ancestor's quest for land, which was a common goal for achievement-oriented men of the middle 1800's. The

United States, and especially within North Carolina, was primarily an agriculturally based economy that relied on land as one of the primary ingredients for success. J. Van started purchasing land on December 12, 1871 when he purchased 92 acres from Emsley Armfield, which included a second tract on the Greensboro to Friendship Road. This was followed by another 51 acres in 1873.

A few years later, on September 2, 1875, J. Van married Lysandra Alethea Ann Cook, more commonly known as Sandia. Like most good Quaker families of the time, they started having one child every two years: their first son Paul Cameron Lindley was born on April 27, 1877 and then came Eva Lindley born on September 30, 1879.

The marriage to Sandia Cook and starting his family provided J. Van with enhanced vigor. Although neither he nor Joshua showed up in Branson's Directory in 1872, sometime between 1874 and 1877 (most references cite 1877 as the year), J. Van started "Pomona Hills Nursery" as this account from a short biography by George Grimsley explains:

> "...he began business as sole proprietor of the Po-
> mona Nursery without other capital than the stock
> of good credit which comes from a long continued
> course of care, promptness and honorable dealing
> and this good credit proved most useful when two
> years later unexpected opposition rose and a com-
> bination was formed against him to meet which it
> was necessary to increase his funds and enlarge his
> business. He borrowed money without difficulty
> and at the end of the year wound up with a larger
> trade and a heavier balance in his favor than ever.
> He did more, not only had he met the opposition
> and won the victory but he had met the enemy and
> won them as friends" (Ashe, Weeks and Van
> Noppen).

Between 1875 and 1881 J. Van's land acquisition plans were in full motion. His land holdings of 143 acres swelled to

839 by June of 1881. He purchased 11 different tracts from the following families in the Friendship/Moorehead districts of Guildford County: Austin, Armfield, Hiatt, Peeples, McCrackin, Joyce, Edwards, Eggert, Meekins and Rainey. The land was on both sides of the North Carolina Railroad and along the "Greensboro to Friendship Road" later known as Spring Garden Street and Muir's Chapel Road.

During this period of land acquisition, J. Van was listed as a "Master" of New Garden Grange [one of ten in Guilford County] in the Directory of the Granges in North Carolina. This was a new agricultural organization organized in 1875 to bring together farmers and provide an advocacy voice. This marked J. Van's first documented participation in an organized professional group. While the impact of the group was brief, it did provide a model for subsequent agricultural groups.

1880-1891

1880 Census

The 1880 Census found J. Van and his family living in Friendship Township, J. Van was 41 by this time, listed as a nurseryman and he lived there with his wife Sandia, age 26, son Paul, age 3, and new daughter Eva. In addition, they had seven other people living with them, all with white skin color, all born in North Carolina from North Carolina parents:

> John W. Ingold, a nurseryman apprentice, age 16,
> Mary Razl, no listed relationship, age 6,
> Mary Cook, single, sister of Sandia, aged 22,
> Emily McCrackin, single, a cook, age 27,
> John Newel, single, a laborer, age 18,
> W. Isaac Stanley, single, a laborer, age 22 and
> A. Norf Dobsen, single, laborer, age 20 (United
> States Government 1880).

Unlike his ancestors, J. Van did not have a large family to work his nurseries. He had to hire his laborers. The post-war economy allowed for him to hire young workers, probably for low wages, but in exchange he had to provide a home and food. The presence of John Ingold as an apprentice may also show that formal schooling was still being put behind work experience, or, since it was summertime, it could have been just a job for the summer.

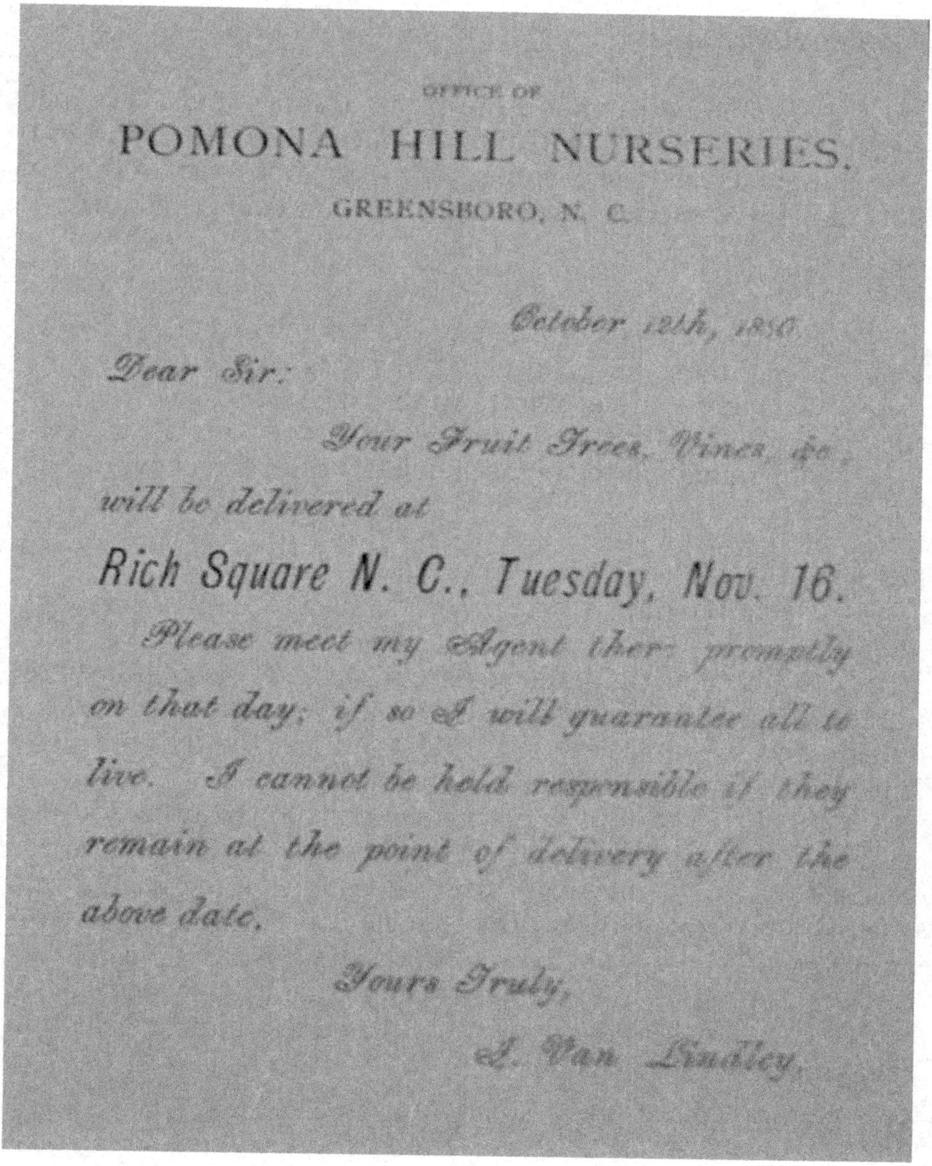

OFFICE OF
POMONA HILL NURSERIES.
GREENSBORO, N. C.

October 12th, 1880.

Dear Sir:

Your Fruit Trees, Vines, &c.,
will be delivered at

Rich Square N. C., Tuesday, Nov. 16.

Please meet my Agent there promptly
on that day; if so I will guarantee all to
live. I cannot be held responsible if they
remain at the point of delivery after the
above date.

Yours Truly,

J. Van Lindley,

Figure 14 - Nursery Correspondence

Pomona Hills Nursery

A simple letter with a pre-printed notice and a stamped addition was found in the Guilford College files of J. Van Lindley. It was written on October 12, 1880 from the "Office of Pomona Hill Nurseries Greensboro, NC" and reads as follows:

Dear Sir:

Your Fruit Trees, Vines, etc. will be delivered at
Rich Square N.C., Tuesday, Nov. 16. Please meet
my Agent there promptly on that day; if so I will
guarantee all to live. I cannot be held responsible if
they remain at the point of delivery after the above
date.

Yours Truly,

J. Van Lindley.

Notice that the letter does not state an exact time. Presumably this is because the agent would be on a train and the schedule was well known, but it does not specify that he will be on a train, stage, or horse-drawn wagon.

Another set of business instructions for planting that his company sent was documented as follows. By reading the words he used to instruct his customers, we can get some insight into how J. Van formed the words that he must have spoken over and over to his many customers. Notice how specific his instructions become, how he emphasizes punctuality and a business-minded approach. Listening carefully, we can almost hear him speaking to us:

J. VAN. LINDLEY, PROPRIETOR.

ADVICE TO PATRONS.

The soil for an orchard should be plowed and
cropped the season previously, and before planting
should be stirred as deeply as possible by means of
a sub-soil plow, having given it a good coat of well

pulverized compost, if the ground is not sufficient-
ly good without it.

If the soil be retentive of moisture, underdraining
should be attended to, as it is impossible to grow
trees with stagnant water about the roots.

PLANTING.

Downing very justly said: "Many persons plant a
tree as they would a post," and one-half of the fail-
ures are in consequence of negligence in this re-
spect. The holes should be dug broader than the
roots extend and a little deeper. With an attendant
to hold the tree, commence filling in the best and
the finest pulverized soil around the roots, at the
same time observing that every rootlet be placed in
its proper position, and in contact with the soil,
and by all means guard against the roots being
matted together. When the hole is partly filled, a
bucket of water may be poured in to settle the soil
firmly and fill the vacancies among the fibers. The
hole may now be filled and trodden lightly.

Never plant a tree more than one or two inches
deeper than it grew in the Nursery, excepting
dwarf pears. The junction of the draft and root
should be three or four inches under the surface of
the ground.

We have seen a very beneficial effect produced on
newly planted trees, particularly during a drought,
by dipping the roots previously to planting in a
thin puddle of mud. This adhering to the small fibers tends to keep them moist for a long time.

After planting, the soil around the tree should be
mulched with leaves, straw, or coarse litter of any
kind, in order to keep the soil from becoming dry
during the summer.

Be careful to stake the trees firmly, and to protect them from rabbits during the winter by wrapping them with some kind of coarse straw, or take a dry cornstalk, split it open, take out the pith, and it will fit nicely around the young tree. Be sure to take them off in the spring, and be sure to remove the wires, as they will impair the tree

ASPARAGUS.—Enrich and stir the ground thoroughly two feet deep, add plenty of decayed manure and loam—the beds cannot be made too rich. Plant in rows, 12 or 15 inches each way, and cover them four to six inches deep with rich loam. Keep the head clean and add a dressing of rich loam and plenty of salt annually in January.

STRAWBERRIES.—Plant in rows from two to three feet, fifteen inches apart. Water and protect from the dew if necessary when first planted. Cultivate well, keep runners clipped and the ground rich if you want fine, large berries. A covering of horse manure in early winter will protect the plants, act as a fertilizer, mulch and keep the berries clean.

PRUNING.

I have frequently advised purchasers on how to prune their trees before planting, but the great majority appear to think it spoils the looks of the tree, and the consequence is, they are never afterwards able to form a finely shaped top.

Before the trees are planted, cut all bruised and broken roots off carefully and smoothly, and trim the branches back from one to two feet, with an eye to forming a regular pyramid-shaped head. The lower branches should be left somewhat longer than those above, and in all cases CUT beyond a bud.

In pruning as the tree increases in age, a judicious thinning of the branches must be attended to, always remembering that none should be removed that will in any way mar the beauty of the tree. The best season for pruning is in the autumn, as the sap goes down, and in the spring as the sap rises; but never prune with a dull knife.

AFTER MANAGEMENT.

If this is not attended to properly, for a few years after planting, a profitable return need not be expected, for nothing is so conducive to the health and strong growth of a tree as to have the surface of the soil cultivated and strictly clean.

All weeds and grass should be carefully avoided. Never crop with sown grain. The best crops for young orchards are corn, potatoes, and all kinds of culinary vegetables, which allow a free use of the cultivator.

SEASON FOR PLANTING.

Transplanting may be successfully performed at any time between the first of November and the first of April, provided the ground is clear of frost and not too wet; but the sooner the better after the first mentioned date, as the earth settles better about the roots than when planted later.

DISTANCE FOR PLANTING.

Standard Apples.............................20 to 50 feet.

Dwarf Apples..................................... 10

Standard Pears.................................. 20

Dwarf Pears...................................... 10

Peaches and Cherries........................ 20

Plums, Apricots and Nectarines.........15 to 20

Grapes... 6 to 8

Strawberries.. 1 by 2

In receipt of your Trees, Vines, etc., do not let
them be exposed, but open the bundle and heel
them in the ground at once, and if well done, they
will keep in your garden, in good condition until
spring; or you can plant at leisure, a few at a time,
during the winter. Should they become dry or
shriveled, soak them in water twenty-four hours
before heeling them in the ground.

Notice. All subscribers for Trees, Vines, etc. will
please meet my Agent promptly on the day appointed. I shall fill all orders in good faith and
shall expect every subscriber to receive his trees.
Remember the day and date given on the back of
this circular and come for your trees accordingly.

The life of business is promptness. I shall endeavor
to properly fill all orders and avoid all mistakes,
but should any occur notice must be given at once
and they will be corrected with pleasure.

Descriptive Catalogues free to applicants.

Respectfully,

J. Van. Lindley.

Greensboro, N. C.

•P. S. If there is anything you wish to add to your
order please notify me at once (University of
Georgia Library).

Growing Family

The year 1881 brought two important family events: his
daughter Pearl Lindley was born on July 28, 1881 and his father
Joshua died during the two months prior to her birth. J. Van
had fulfilled his last obligation to his father by helping him
achieve financial solvency and was now mid-way through forming his family. His family would be completed during the ensu-

ing ten years, with the additions of Cammie Gozeal Lindley, born on October 11, 1883, then Mary Judith Lindley born August 8, 1885, and finally Annie Marie Lindley born July 6, 1891. All of these children lived full lives except Mary Judith. She lived just over one year and died on January 31, 1887. The cause of her death is not known, but the young death of his fifth child added another tragedy to his life, but one that did not alter J. Van's enduring determination.

Figure 15 - 1886 Pomona Hills Advertisement

Guilford College Trustee

In 1885 J. Van became a Trustee of the New Garden
Boarding School at Guilford and helped guide it through the
transition in 1888 when it changed its name to Guilford College
and significantly expanded its course offerings. He serving
continuously on the board until his death in 1918, adding up to a
total service of 33 years, one of the longest terms served by any
trustee of the institution. As his 33 years of service attest, J. Van
became passionate about education and he put his drive and
efforts into making sure future generations would receive the
full benefits of a robust education; despite the fact that he was
only able to get a small sample.

Research at Guilford College's Library into his role in
promoting the transition to a college, building the physical
buildings on campus, fund-raising and leaving a large endowment with very little debt is summarized in the following ex-
tracts from the research:

> The Executive Committee of the Yearly Meeting
> considered on July 2, 1873...an endorsement of a
> plan to make a first-class college at new Garden.
> The "College at New Garden" to which the commit-
> tee referred did not come into being until 15 years
> later, but the endorsement and improvement of
> the boarding school soon came, it largely due to
> the efforts of Francis J. King with the backing and
> support of the Baltimore Association.

On October 1, 1885 the Board of Trustees at New Garden
Boarding School started a notebook entitled "subscriptions and
receipts of money for rebuilding at new Garden." The first set of
entries is titled "collections after June 1, 1887."

Within the notes of the Board of Trustees, listed as investments of endowment for 1896, one of the line items says J.
Van Lindley $1836.40. It is not clear whether this is a donation
by J. Van Lindley or if this was investment by the endowment
fund in one of J. Van Lindley's enterprises.

The first mention of an accounting for the balance of an endowment fund is in the yearly meeting minutes for 1897 on page 31 where it states that the endowment income is stated as $1532.25. In 1898 the income from the endowment was $1317.91.

On page 54 of this notebook is a series of subscriptions titled "subscriptions made from January 16 to June 1, 1904 to clear the college of debt. John V. Lindley is listed as the second donor with a donation of $1500. On page 60 is a record of the Guilford College general endowment for the year 1905. Along with others, Andrew Carnegie donated $45,000 to this fund and JB and BN Duke donated $15,000. J. Van Lindley donated $1500, which made him the seventh largest donor that year.

On September 18, 1918, a few months after J. Van Lindley's death, the Board of Trustees reported that the endowment investments totaled $193,826.18. With low debt and a large endowment, J. Van had left Guilford College in much better position than when he first became involved in 1885.

The book <u>Guilford a Quaker College</u> by Dorothy Gilbert covers much of the school's history and includes several pertinent comments concerning J. Van's involvement as a trustee:

> Guilford has been fortunate in her trustees; often they have lent the continuity and stability necessary to the well-being of any school in which the students and teachers support according to the laws of periodicity and chance... the custom has been for trustees to recommend a committeeman to the yearly meeting; it confirms their appointment; then the board elects him as a trustee. Since 1905, when the charter was amended, trustees serve six-year terms but usually succeed themselves. The system has given the school and the college a succession of interested trustees, each servant over a period of years... John Van Lindley... served for 30 years or more.

> In the summer of 1908 founders Hall was remodeled. In 1909 the library was finished in Kane Hall

started, in 1910 the present King Hall was completed and plans for Cox all announced. The trustees presented a masterly summary of the past and
a forecast of the future in the 1910 report. Said
they: "since last yearly meeting the library building
has been completed. King Hall has been rebuilt,
the debt of one year ago has been reduced to about
$5000, and the assets of the college had been in-
creased to a little more than $30,000. We have for
several years hope to see the time, when we would
be able to erect a new, up-to-date and adequate
dormitory building for boys. This building is badly
needed and we feel that the time has come for us
to begin this work, and we trust that every friend
of the institution will assist us in this, our next un-
dertaking."

The trustees who felt the urgency of their task and
built as steadily as Noah before the flood were...
[including] John Van Lindley... special building
committees bore much of the burden in the heat of
the period...(Thorne).

Pomona Terra-Cotta

J. Van's business grew steadily during the 1880's and in
1886, on a list of Guilford County land owners, he was listed as
owning 754 acres, making him the 39th largest landowner in the
county and in the top 2% in terms of size of holdings [a detailed
review of purchases and sales by J. Van Lindley in the Guildford
County records differs from this account, as the total of his land
equaled over 1000 acres starting early in 1886]. Up to this point,
J. Van had only focused on being a nurseryman and, except for
being on the Board of Trustees, had not ventured outside the
agricultural field.

J. Van's first venture outside agriculture came in 1886
when Angus M. Smith, a mining engineer from New York,
approached J. Van about starting a small terra-cotta plant on a
nearby farm that included clay deposits. J. Van realized that

there was a need for controlled water drainage systems for his and other nurseries. Also, Angus probably told him about the first city to get a sewer system, Brooklyn in 1857, and that it would eventually be coming to the South. Indoor plumbing was just becoming a reality in New York, but was in its infancy in North Carolina. Despite the venture being outside of his expertise, J. Van was open-minded enough to listen, reason, embrace the cause, and put his efforts into turning the business into a success.

The two formalized an agreement on July 14, 1886 when they held a stockholder's meeting where Angus received 24 shares and J. Van Lindley received 24 shares. Angus was elected President and J. Van Lindley was elected Secretary. The next month they met at Porter & Dalton's Drug Store and agreed to order Davis' "Practical Treatise on the Manufacture of Bricks, Tiles, Terra-Cotta, Etc." During the first quarter of 1887, they offered 12 shares of stock to raise more capital. Angus ran the company during the first year and by the end of that year, the company had lost money. Angus left at the end of this first year and J. Van bought out Angus's shares (Meeker).

At that point, according to Grimsley's short biography, written in 1905:

> Mr. Lindley with his usual foresight and good
> business judgment prompted by inherent ambition
> to succeed in whatever he undertook bought the
> plant in 1890 [according to the company records
> this would have been 1887] and equipped it with
> the best machinery that could be purchased. In
> three years he had made such a gratifying success
> of it that he doubled the capacity of the plant and
> began the manufacture of sewer pipes, drain tiles,
> firebrick and chimney flues. The Pomona Terra
> Cotta Works now [by 1905] have a capacity of one
> hundred and sixteen [rail] cars per month and
> cannot supply the demand (Ashe, Weeks and Van
> Noppen).

When Angus left, J. Van Lindley became President of the fledgling company and served until January 28, 1907. Just as importantly, Charles Boren, who had been involved from the beginning in helping to run the business, remained. The Boren family soon got more involved in the running, ownership, and success that followed. Charles was elected to the Board of Directors on July 15, 1889 at the annual meeting. By January 16, 1905, when a stockholder's meeting increased the capital stock from $25,000 to $50,000 several Boren family members controlled a combined 120 of the 250 shares and J. Van Lindley owned 80 shares. Interrelated marriages between the Lindley, Cook, Hunt and Boren families combined for almost all of the shares, making it more of a family business (Meeker).

Day-to-day, the Boren family members clearly had responsibility for and control of the company. They held most of the key management positions as time went on. At its height, this company employed 300-400 North Carolinians and supplied their full line of terra cotta products, particularly sewer pipes, across North Carolina and to other Southern cities.

This taste for something new emboldened J. Van even further. He became the Postmaster for Pomona, serving from May 26, 1886 to August 31, 1903. Approaching age 50, he also expanded his operations in 1887 by building the first commercial range of greenhouses in the area. He built them on land originally known as Salem Junction, but later changed to a name his father would have appreciated - Pomona.

Cherokee Descendent

On a more personal note, J. Van Lindley filed a legally certified document with the U.S. Government in October of 1887 where he attested to being of Cherokee descent. This was due to an Act of Congress on February 8, 1887 named: An Act to Provide for the Allotment of Lands in Severalty to Indians on the Various Reservations (General Allotment Act or Dawes Act). The act granted a one-quarter section of land (160 acres) to each certified head of household on Indian reservations. He was able to make his claim because his Great Grandmother was ½ Cherokee Indian, his Grandmother 1/4, his Mother 1/8, and he was 1/16 Cherokee Indian. Enrollment in the Eastern Band of Cherokee Indians today is governed by Cherokee Code, Chapter 49, Enrollment, and restricts enrollment to the following: direct lineal ancestor must appear on the 1924 Baker Roll of the Eastern Band of Cherokee Indians and must possess at least 1/16 degree of Eastern Cherokee blood. The reason for his taking this action was probably because if any of J. Van Lindley's children had applied for Cherokee citizenship and lived on the land for 25 years, they would have been given clear title to the land (none took advantage of this opportunity).

1890 Census

The 1890 United States Census was taken during the month of June, 1890. Unfortunately, the records were destroyed by a fire in the basement of the U.S. Commerce Building, thereby not allowing access to census records for that decade.

American Association of Nurserymen

During mid-summer 1890, J. Van attended the fifteenth annual meeting of the American Association of Nurserymen in New York City. While there are no records indicating prior attendance, he may have been a member and attended previous meetings because at the June meeting he was elected First Vice-President. The following year the meeting was held in Minneapolis and he spoke about the "Fruit Culture in North Carolina." At the latter meeting, he was elected President of the organization for 1891-1892. These meetings allowed J. Van to travel to larger cities, but more importantly to meet with other nurserymen and hear their vibrant discussions about subjects important to him. Nurserymen from the North were very interested in business opportunities in the South. The profit potential of orchards verses selling nursery stock was debated. The cost and logistics of rail freight was also discussed. In a very rare event, J. Van the Quaker, known for being quiet, was recorded at the 1891 meeting making the following remarks, which show us how he presented himself to a group of his peers through these recorded words:

> "The President : ...The secretary informs me that Mr. Berckmans has been unable to be present, and we hope that Mr. Van Lindley, or other representative men of the South will respond verbally upon the condition of our industry in that section. I will call upon Mr. Van Lindley to make a few remarks if he will.
>
> Mr. Van Lindley : I am not like Mr. Hale, I was not cut out as a speaker, and I always dread to get up before an audience. At the same time, in North Carolina I have seen the nursery business from its infancy; I may say back forty years. I can say, my father at one time ran the largest nursery business in that country, hauled his trees off in wagons and dealt them out. I suppose he raised 10,000 a year, that was a big thing in those days, at least he thought it was a big business, and it was a pretty good business at that time. I suppose that I grow about as many trees in a year as he did in a lifetime. You can tell by that whether or not it is increasing in that country. You may not believe it, but I am informed by good authority, that in the south today is one of the largest nurseries in the world [here J. Van is referring indirectly to his own nursery], and in a state where there were no nurseries 25 years ago worth mentioning. In other states during the past ten years the industry built up at such a rate that if it goes on 20 years longer it will be ahead of the eastern nurseries, or at least it looks so at the present day.
>
> Now, there are a few parties who want me to say a little about the great freeze we had in our country this past spring. Several have asked me whether they had any fruit down there. I do not know how

many. I always make the inquiry, " Do you ever
read anything ?" It has been thoroughly published
all over the country and I thought nurserymen
were readers, and it is something amazing to me to
hear them ask such questions. I shall not give away
any of the names, whatever I say about them.

A Member : We want to get it straight.

Mr. Van Lindley: Well now the freeze itself was not
remarkable, but the season is what did it. I will
give you some idea of what kind of season we had.
In February it was unusually warm, quite so that
all early fruits such as apricots and peaches were
out in bloom by the last of the month. We had a little cold spell in the latter part of February, but it
did not get very cold, not enough to injure the
fruit; then March came in as warm as August, I
suppose, in New York, and remained so over three
weeks, till the 25th of March.

During that time we were busy with our nursery
work in that country. Everything was starting just
as rapidly as it well could under the circumstances,
plenty of rain, and the thermometer running up
about 80 to 90, and you know how things grow in
that condition. All the planting was done, peach
buds were headed back, starting out; young Kieffer
pears growing from 6 to 15 inches. Take the fruit in
that condition and on the morning of the 26th of
March, at 9 o'clock, the thermometer commenced
to fall, starting from 80. It went in the course of
about twelve hours down to 26. It might have been
70 to 26. Next morning the thermometer regis-
tered 20 above zero ; the third morning it was 18,
so you can judge from the degree of cold the condition we were in at the end of the third day, or even
at the second.

You know what would be the result if you were to
open a greenhouse here in this climate in mid-

winter. Everything was killed down; all shrubs, roses, and many of the kinds of shrubs that I never saw hurt before. Kieffer pear trees—I had quite a number of trees that have been bearing at least ten years—all the top had to come off. We cut off the tops as far as they were blackened, and they are growing out beautifully now, and in a year from now you will hardly be able to tell that they have been frozen. But young stock, like the Kieffer pears, anywhere under three years old, were killed to the ground ; all have to be cut down under the surface; and in some locations down there old peach trees were killed, and the nursery stock that suffered mostly was peach buds that had been cut back and had already been sold.

Peach stock in that part of the country was nearly all killed. Peach seedlings that were up were killed to the ground. I had started the finest peach seed-lings I ever had, and apple seedlings that high, and they were all killed; so were our pear seedlings. That is about the condition of things all through the Piedmont section. I do not know how far it ex-tends west, hardly, but such a freeze was never known in that country before, unless it was in 1846.

I recollect father talking about a freeze when I was a boy, that took place in '40, or after '40, but the results were about the same, I think from what I can find out, for I remember he showed me per-simmons trees of which the tops were dead, and said that was caused by the late freeze in '46. So we are not apt to see such a freeze as that more than once in a lifetime, if we do that" (American Association of Nurserymen).

Peach Orchard near Southern Pines

Upon returning from these meetings in 1890, J. Van began to expand his participation in activities beyond his nursery. Although Branson's 1890 business listings show him as a "Farmer" under both Greensboro and Salem Junction, he was becoming much more active. Perhaps because of what he learned at the national meetings, in 1891 he ambitiously began purchasing property in Greensboro, NC and near Southern Pines, NC in Moore County. He had very definite plans for each parcel. He incorporated a company in 1891, which he named the J. Van Lindley Orchard Company. He then bought 750 acres, another 346 acres, and 3 lots near Southern Pines, NC. The combined acreage became a peach orchard containing 50,000 peach trees in rows 1 ½ miles long. He spent the entire year setting up 500 acres of peaches in his new orchard (Carpenter and Colvard).

Continuing the expansion of his activities beyond the orchards, J. Van also represented the 5th District at the NC State Agricultural Society and became a charter member of the Greensboro MM after having attended the New Garden MM for most of his life.

Greensboro Becomes a Key Rail Hub

By 1891 there were 16 major manufacturing plants in the city of Greensboro. Railroad development continued and there were lines running east to west, north to south, southeast to northwest and west to Winston. The arrival and departure of 60 trains a day gave Greensboro its nickname the "Gate City" in 1891 and provided ample transportation opportunities for the Pomona Hills Nursery. The result was an expansion of potential business customers to a 500-mile radius in all directions, putting most of the east coast of the United States within reach.

Figure 16 - J. Van Lindley Nursery, Pomona, NC

1892: Trip to Europe

Trip to Europe and the Middle East

At the end of 1891, J. Van's good friend Addison Coffin returned from Indiana with an ambitious plan. Addison, who was also the first cousin of J. Van's deceased first wife Mary Coffin, had decided to travel to the Middle East and Europe sometime during 1892. After meeting a Quaker missionary who was headed to England in early February, he was convinced to speed up his departure plans and accompany her and her friend on the voyage. Like J. Van, Addison was a multi-talented man. Addison was much older than J. Van and had already grown up in Greensboro, moved to Indiana, raised a family, survived the death of two wives, and travelled extensively guiding settlers westward while he provided advice to them on where to locate and purchase property. He had been successful at this and now wanted to see the other parts of the world which he had not visited.

After getting his nursery, terra cotta pipe making company and extensive peach orchard started, J. Van made the sudden and startling decision that he would accompany Addison on the journey. Fortunately, Addison Coffin wrote a book published in 1897 that recorded this trip in detail. The name of the book is Life And Times of Addison Coffin By Himself.

A detailed account of their trip takes up chapters nine through twelve in the book, beginning at page 271 and continuing until page 472. The two travelled almost continuously for the entire nine-month period. J. Van was 53 at this time and Addison was 69. An outline with a very short narrative of their trip follows (dates appear when they were mentioned in the text). The two hundred and one page version written by Addison Coffin contains fascinating observations, is surprisingly easy to read and entertaining [the web address for an online version can be found in the bibliography under "Coffin"] (Coffin).

A copy of J. Van Lindley's Passport Application mentions that he would return to the United States "within 2 years," an indication that it might not have been entirely clear how long a trip like this might take. Guilford County records also list a Power of Attorney document with Charles Boren taking over full responsibility for keeping up his business interests during the absence.

The first part of their trip took the pair of older men from New York City to Liverpool, England. This part of the trip got them close to the departure point for their European trips, which was London, England.

Trip to New York, NY - 1892

Greensboro - February 8
Washington DC

Atlantic Crossing — February, 1892

New York, New York — February 12
Crossing of Atlantic Ocean - February 13
Liverpool, England — February 23

Their first big excursion was to the Middle East. Both were very well versed in biblical training and lore. They were keen to see where the events of the Bible had occurred. They took a few extra days on the way to see several of the European capitals, and then went straight to the pyramids in Egypt. Their time in Palestine (now Israel) was more leisurely as they walked around Jerusalem and to the nearby towns and sites that played such an important part in Christ's life and the events of the Bible. They spent about 5 weeks on this section of the journey.

Trip to Egypt

London, England
Paris, France
Rome, Italy
Naples, Italy
Crossing of the Mediterranean Sea
Alexandria, Egypt — March 4
Cairo, Egypt
Ismalia, Egypt
Port Said, Egypt

Trip to Palestine

Mediterranean Sea
Jaffa, Palestine (Tel Aviv, Israel)
Ramlah, Palestine
Jerusalem
Jericho
Dead Sea
Jacobs Crossing
Jerusalem
Bethlehem
Mount of Olives
Jaffa, Palestine

Trip to Lebanon & Syria

Mediterranean Sea
Beirut, Lebanon
Damascus, Syria
Mt. Lebanon, Lebanon - March 26
Beirut, Lebanon - April 5

After sightseeing in the Middle East, they returned in such a way as to visit most of the major capitals of Europe. They had the opportunity and the means to take the Orient Express, which had begun operating only a few years earlier. Instead, the pair decided to take the slowest trains possible, traveling during the day and staying in a different city each night. They enjoyed watching the countryside go by at speeds of 18 miles per hour, about the same speed as a fast bicycle. They began in Greece and Turkey, took railroad cars all the way back to France, and stopped in the major towns. They then crossed the English Channel in time to get to the Quaker Annual Meeting in London. This part of the trip took them another 5 weeks.

Trip to Greece

Crossing of Mediterranean Sea
Island of Cyprus
Island of Patmos
Island of Rhodes
Athens, Greece

Trip across Europe

Crossing of Mediterranean Sea
Constantinople, Turkey (Istanbul)
Through Bulgaria
Through Romania
Belgrade, Serbia
Budapest, Hungary
Vienna, Austria
Linz, Austria
Nürnberg, Germany
Frankfurt, Germany
Bonn, Germany
Brussels, Belgium
Calais, France
Crossing of English Channel
Dover, England
London, England

The Yearly Quaker Meeting was an important event for ardent Quakers. Having the ability to attend the London meeting was special because the Quaker movement started in England and, although many left due to persecution, it was still the center of the Quaker world and, due to the dominance at the time of the British Empire, the crossroads of the worldwide Quaker movement. They spent about 3 weeks attending these meetings.

London Yearly Quaker Meeting - May 18

The next journey took them to Scandinavian countries, but then spread well beyond as they traveled across to Moscow, then took the arduous journey back across Europe down to Spain and Portugal. They then doubled back across Spain and up through France due to a mix-up with tickets, and finally returned to London. This part of the trip completed an "X" across Europe, with their first trip starting in the southeast corner and coming to the northwest and the second (starting from Moscow) starting in the northeast corner and then coming down to the southwest. This approach, supplemented by a trip across the bottom to the Middle East and across the top from Scandinavia to Moscow, very effectively covered all of Europe. This section of the trip covered a 6-7 week time period.

Trip to Scandinavian countries

London, England - June 3
Norwich, England
Crossing of English Channel
Rotterdam, Netherlands
Bremen, Germany
Hamburg, Germany
Kiel, Germany - June 7
Crossing of Baltic Sea
Korsor, Denmark
Copenhagen, Denmark
Helsingor, Denmark
Christiana, Norway (Oslo)

Stockholm, Sweden - June 12
Haparanda, Sweden - June 15
Tornio, Finland
Umea, Sweden
Lulea, Sweden - June 18
Uleaborg, Finland - June 23
Vassa, Finland

Trip to Russia

Vyborg, Russia
St. Petersburg, Russia
Moscow, Russia

Second trip across Europe

Warsaw, Poland
Berlin, Germany
Munich, Germany
Venice, Italy
Milan, Italy
Lucerne, Switzerland
Berne, Switzerland
Geneva, Switzerland
Lyon, France
Montpelier, France
Irun, Spain
Madrid, Spain
Lisbon, Portugal
Porto, Portugal
Bordeaux, France
Orleans, France
Angers, France
Saint-Malo, France
Crossing of English Channel
Jersey Island, UK
Guernsey Island, UK
Weymouth, UK
London, UK

The pair rested briefly in London, then took the last major leg of their journey. The physical stamina and high energy exhibited by these men of advanced age as they continued to explore these foreign lands month after month is impressive. Their trip was to Wales, Ireland, Scotland and northern England. It started with them taking a train across southern England, through Wales, and then travelling by ferry across the Irish Sea. Once in Ireland, they started in Dublin and worked their way clockwise around the elongated island, up the western coast, and back eastward to Northern Ireland, ending in Belfast. From there they took the ferry over to Glasgow, Scotland and continued their clockwise movement, but now moving down the larger United Kingdom island through York and back to London. They moved rather rapidly on this part, as they were covering fewer miles, and finished the section in 3 weeks.

Trip to Ireland — August 5

London, UK
Bristol, UK
Tintern Abbey, Wales
Liverpool, UK
Crossing of Irish Sea
Dublin, Ireland
Portarlington, Ireland
Kilkenny, Ireland
Waterford, Ireland
Killarney Lake, Ireland
Tralee, Ireland
Limerick, Ireland
Ennis, Ireland
Athenry, Ireland
Athlone, Ireland
Mullingar, Ireland
Sligo, Ireland

Trip to Northern Ireland

Enniskillen, No. Ireland
Londonderry, No. Ireland

Portsteward, No. Ireland
Giant's Causeway, No. Ireland
Lake Neagh, No. Ireland
Carrickfergus, No. Ireland
Balynalinch, No. Ireland
Belfast, No. Ireland

Trip to Scotland

Crossing of Irish Sea
Port Glasgow, Scotland
Glasgow, Scotland
Loch Lomond, Scotland
Stirling, Scotland
Dunblane, Scotland
Perth, Scotland
Dundee, Scotland
Edinburgh, Scotland
Annan, Scotland
Gretna, Scotland
Newcastle, UK
York, UK
London, UK — August 24

At the end of their trip, they again boarded a passenger line that carried them from England back to New York. Lest we think that travel at that time was predictable, the tale of their return was harrowing, especially being adrift for 3 days without any means of propulsion. Their trip across the Atlantic to England had likewise been marked by an emergency incident where members of their ship had to save men from another vessel that was damaged by a rough Atlantic storm. J. Van Lindley and Addison Coffin returned not shell-shocked by the potential tragedies, but invigorated by all they had seen and experienced. J. Van's greatest years, possibly inspired by this trip, lay ahead, and Addison would continue travelling for several more years before writing his autobiography (Coffin).

Figure 17 - J. Van Lindley - 1892

1893 - 1905: Entrepreneur

Southern Pines Orchard Development

Upon returning from his European trip in late 1892, J. Van resumed work developing his orchards in Southern Pines. Acreage was quoted as being sold at the time for from 50 cents to one dollar per acre, with thousands of acres being available. These light, sandy soils were judged to be too dry for producing plant material suitable for animal grazing, and animal manure was not available for fertilization. The use of commercial fertilizers seemed to be the only practical approach to profitable production, but they were too expensive for the row crops that could be grown in the soil.

As President of the North Carolina Horticulture Society, J. Van worked specifically to solve the problem of how to best utilize and develop the land in the Sandhills region of North Carolina. He set up a partnership with the newly organized Department of Plant Biology at NC State University. Together, they moved the North Carolina Agricultural Experiment Station from Raleigh to land he donated to the partnership in Southern Pines. As described by the university:

> "The objective of the research was to determine the proportion of the different fertilizing ingredients necessary and the optimum soil treatment needed to obtain the best growth and development of orchard and garden fruits and other horticultural and agricultural products.

> A six-member supervising committee was appointed to carry out the work. H.B. Battle (whose father Kemp Battle, President of UNC and sometimes called the "father of the experiment station") was the Director of the Experiment Station from 1887 to 1897. Wilbur Fiske Massey, one of the first five professors at NC State, also represented the experiment station. From the Horticultural Society, J. Van Lindley, President, C.D. Tarbell, a mem-

ber of the executive committee of the society; and
Michael McCarthy, secretary of the society and also station researcher, were included. B. Von Herff,
an assistant chemist with the station from 1883
until 1887, represented the German Kali Works.
D.D.F. Cameron was selected as farm superintendent. Wilbur Fiske Massey moved much of his research from Raleigh to Southern Pines."

The J. Van Lindley Orchard Company undoubtedly bene-
fited from the research. In 1897 the company realized $8,063.51
net profit from the peach orchard's first crop. J. Van was quoted
as saying that he: "considers it only about 1/8 of what the crop
would be when the trees had full age." For an investment in
inexpensive land, the profits were large with the possibility of
being much larger.

The work with the station went on for several years before ending in 1898 due to a political change resulting in Michael McCarthy losing his position. This was unfortunate
because McCarthy had been instrumental in integrating ento-
mology and botany interests, specifically fighting the infesta-
tions that destroyed crops. The very next year the San Jose scale,
a sucking insect that injected a toxin into the fruit plants causing
a bright red fruit discoloration and white speckled damage to
the trees, spread across the peach trees in the state.

Unfortunately, the San Jose scale infestation of 1899
forced the J. Van Lindley Orchard Company into an economic
tailspin. J. Van, in a private letter to W. J. Peele in April of 1899,
blamed the devastation as coming directly from Professor
Massey discharging Professor McCarthy. J. Van felt that McCarthy had been an active entomologist who was successfully
cleaning out the San Jose scale prior to being removed from his
position (J. V. Lindley). J. Van had reason to be upset because
all of his orchard trees had to be cut down and replanted. When
the other investors decided to get out, J. Van Lindley bought
their shares and continued pursuing the opportunity. In the
early 1900's, a successful treatment to stop the San Jose scale

was finally found, allowing J. Van Lindley's orchards to return to healthy production.

The significance of J. Van Lindley's leadership in the area of peach research was two-fold:

> First, prior to his involvement, state researchers and growers recognized that it was not yet possible to profitably grow peaches in the Sandhills region of North Carolina, and

> Second, he managed to create a partnership between researchers, growers, and a fertilizer company to cooperatively solve this problem.

As one historian commented: "As far as now can be determined, that project [referring to the J. Van Lindley Peach Orchard] was the first critical step in the development of the peach orchard industry that in the years afterward prospered and enriched local counties" (Arnett).

Southern Pines Land Purchases and Sales

During the 1890's J. Van Lindley proved out his concept by buying lots and building packing, warehousing and shipping operations in nearby Southern Pines. He also worked out an arrangement for the trolley line that ran between the Southern Pines train station and the newly formed town of Pinehurst to extend a spur out to his peach orchard. This trolley was utilized almost full-time during the peach-picking season to get the product to the train station from the orchard.

A summary of his land purchases and (for ease of giving a complete accounting of this subject) sales follows:

> April 1891: Buys 3 lots in Southern Pines for $300 from the New England Mining, Mfg., & Estate Company plus 750 acres from Benjamin Douglass, Jr. For $1,750 ($2.33/acre) and 346 acres from B. Van Hoff for $1038 ($3.00/acre) = 1096 acres.

Jan 1894: Buys 2 lots in Southern Pines for $400

Mar 1895: Buys a small tract for $100 in Southern Pines

Jun 1895: buys 2 lots in Southern Pines for $400

Oct 1895: buys 1335 acres = 2431 acres

Dec 1899: Sells 2 lots for $400

Oct 1916: Sells 400 acres to John Patrick for $10

Sep 1918: Sells 1104 acres for $10,000 and deeds 258.51 acres to PC Lindley

May 1919: Sells 252.08 acres for a cumulative total of 2014 acres sold (416.41 acres were not accounted for by recorded sales)

Apr 1921: Sells remaining Lots in Southern Pines (Moore County)

Figure 18 - Conkleton Pear

The Conkleton Pear

One of J. Van's longer lasting pomological achievements occurred on September 7, 1897. On that date Deborah G. Passmore, a renowned fruit artist, completed a painting of the Conkleton, thereby documenting for the United States Department of Agriculture that J. Van was the original cultivator of this variety (Taylor, 1902). This pear was grown by J. Van Lindley from the seedling of a Le Conte which was a hybrid pear created by growing European and Oriental pears.

Expansion of Business and Philanthropic Interests

Beginning in 1896, the Raleigh News and Observer took over Branson's State Directory. J. Van Lindley was listed many times in this and subsequent annual publications. He was listed in Pomona, North Carolina as owning a nursery and a general store (the Lindley Store Co.) and in Moore County as the J. Van Lindley Orchard Company with 350 acres under cultivation (60,000 trees). In 1901, this same publication changed its name to the North Carolina Yearbook and Business Directory.

From 1901-1916 J. Van Lindley was listed as the President of the N.C. Horticulture Society and a member of its executive committee. In 1902 he was president of the Southern Nurserymen's Association. The same year he became a founding board member of the Children's Home Society. He also leased 26 acres to the Greensboro Streetcar Company to build an amusement park with streetcar access, plus he donated 60 acres of land along Spring Garden Street in Greensboro for a recreation complex that included a man-made lake. He began being listed in 1901 as having a florist business and insurance business named the Security Life and Annuity Company of Greensboro.

In the Spring of 1904 he expanded yet again, developing a 350 acre nursery in Kernersville, NC, adding Forsyth Bank & Trust the next year while simultaneously becoming Vice President of City National Bank in Greensboro (Branson & Farrar).

J. Van Lindley ended 1905 with substantial business interests in Nurseries, Terra Cotta Manufacturing, Orchards,

Florists, Banking, and Insurance entities. His nurseries advertised over 1.5 million plants. Although he was done building his base of business interests, he had only begun to build out the potential for several of his new business ventures. With all of this activity and success, what type of man was he? A short excerpt written for the N.C. Agricultural Society at the time helps best describe him:

> Mr. Lindley is one of the Executive Committee of the North Carolina Agricultural Society and is stockholder in many other industrial organizations. He is thus interested in many enterprises of importance and his name is identified with every undertaking that conduces in any way to the growth in prosperity and in the material and intellectual advancement of the community in which he lives.
>
> Yet among his multifarious interests first in his heart are the nurseries at Pomona, 900 acres in one block devoted to trees and young plants including eleven greenhouses for flowers. Also, 350 acres in nursery at Kernersville, North Carolina, a branch nursery started in the spring of 1904 while at Southern Pines and at other points he has large orchards. Still he finds time to attend national and local meetings of horticulturists and pomologists and he has been prominent in making the fight against the diseases that threaten the gardens. Withal he is quiet and unassuming, prompt and careful. Indeed, he attributes his success in life to his careful attention to every detail of his varied business and he finds great gratification in the fact that he has been able to promote the progress and welfare of that section of the country in which he lives as well as the State at large (Ashe, Weeks and Van Noppen 227).

Southern Nurserymen's Association

After the Civil War, the northern nurserymen dominated the nursery trade and controlled the main trade association, the American Association of Nurserymen. Several of the southern nurserymen, seeking to focus more intently on southern interests and opportunities, started their own association in 1899. J. Van Lindley was President of the association in 1902, followed by his business manager O. Joe Howard in 1913 and 1923. His son Paul C. Lindley was President as well in 1921 (Southern Nursery Association).

Good Roads Club of Guilford County

Prior to the advent of the automobile, roads throughout the south were primarily locally maintained dirt roads. A few toll roads were made with wooden planks that allowed for more reliable travel in poor conditions due to rain or snow. As previously noted, roads were not reliable during the winter months.

According to the "Good Roads Magazine" the "Good Roads" movement began in about 1894 in New Jersey and spread through the northeast. J. Van Lindley is credited in 1899 with leading the way in Guilford County by spearheading the formation of the "Good Roads Club." The purpose of this group was to insure that publicly financed decent thoroughfares be built.

Road legislation began with the Mecklenburg Plan, which one-third of the counties adopted in 1901. The next year a "Good Roads train" crossed North Carolina. The Central Carolina Fair of 1902 featured demonstrations of road building. The North Carolina Good Roads Association was formally organized on February 12 and 13 of 1902. The group then raised a $300,000 bond and established the Guilford Highway Commission. These efforts eventually led today to the establishment of the North Carolina State Highway Commission. By 1910 there were 99 miles of hard surface roads in Guilford County (Good Roads Magazine) (Salsi).

Electric Trolley Cars and Lindley Park

The Greensboro Electric Company, financed by New York investors, began electric streetcar service on June 11, 1902. This service eventually covered 12 miles of track with 24 trolley cars and replaced a small horse drawn trolley car operation. In 1911, the Greensboro Patriots, a minor league professional baseball team, helped to boost trolley popularity with fans riding the trolley to baseball games at Summit Avenue. Other destinations on the trolley included: downtown Greensboro, Lindley Park, the Pomona area, and many new suburban neighborhoods.

Entries in the diary of Mary Kelly Watson Smith referenced two events at Lindley Park, helping to highlight how it was utilized as a center for community activities:

> The first one on September 19, 1907 tells about activities: "The [not intelligible] given by the Civic League at Lindley Park commenced tonight. Entertainment of all sorts" (Smith 153).

> The second entry in 1919 notes: "Lindley Park open for dancing" (Smith 156).

A second item found among the archive clippings kept by the Greensboro Historical Museum about the Lindley family gives further description:

> "Lindley Park-at the southwestern terminus of the electric railway, two and one-half miles from the city, comprises a beautiful tract of twenty-six acres of land, well shaded in native trees; also fine springs of water, a large artificial lake for boating, a neat casino and dance pavilion-all lighted with incandescent electric lamps. This is an ideal place for health or pleasure seekers, and adjoins the far-famed nurseries and greenhouses of J. Van Lindley, whose reputation as a nurseryman and florist is generally known by the lovers of fruits and flowers. He donated the land for this park, and the

electric company did wisely in thus perpetuating
his generosity by naming the park after him."

When the lake and amusement park closed in 1917, the
City hired Earle Sumner Draper to design a planned neighborhood development and what followed was the Lindley Park
neighborhood. His firm, based in Charlotte, NC, created many of
the planned neighborhoods in Charlotte. Many original design
elements of Lindley Park still remain intact today, including the
stone column entryways and tree-lined streets (City of
Greensboro).

Land Purchases, Incorporation and Consolidation of Land Holdings in Pomona

J. Van Lindley made extensive purchases of property pri-
or to the summer of 1899. The following is a summary of the
individual purchases, with a short description (including notation of any along the North Carolina Railroad {NCRR}) to help
in understanding the extent of his passion for acquiring real
estate:

> 1871 - bought 2 tracts of 76 and 16 acres for a total
> of 92 acres from Emsley Armfield for $850
>
> 1873 - bought 51 acres from William Edwards for
> $200 and leased 70 acres from Emily Austin for 3
> years at a cost of $25/year, planted 3000 peach
> and apple trees
>
> 1876 - bought 77.5 acres from Emsley Armfield for
> $271
>
> 1878 - bought 2 tracts of 100 and 18 acres for a to-
> tal of 118 acres from the Hiatt family for $1000
>
> 1878 - bought 2 tracts of land 5.5 and 11 acres for a
> total of 16.5 acres from Emsley Armfield and
> James Joyce for $525
>
> 1878 - bought 70 acres from Emily Austin for $500

1878 - bought 2 acres for $90 from Allen Peeples (along NCRR)

1880 - bought 1 acre for $20 from Julius Meekins (along NCRR)

1880 - bought 200 acres from George Eggert for $950 (along NCRR)

1881 - bought 143 acres from DS Rainey for $1050

1883 - bought 89.25 acres from Siddons, Ridge, Peter Adams (70 acres), and Gosset (no price listed)

1885 - bought 2 acres from Eli Townsend (along NCRR) for $11

1886 - bought 40 acres from Robert Scott for $700 and 188 acres from Joseph Blemer for $1,500

1897 - bought 2 tracts of 221 and 5 acres for a total of 226 acres from Jane Armfield and Thomas Hill for $5,825, paying $1025 up front, with $4500 due Dec 1, 1897

1898 - bought 345 acres from Thomas Willis next to Pomona Terra Cotta for $6,000

...For a cumulative total of about 1667 acres at the end of 1898.

1899 – J. Van Lindley incorporated his holdings into J. Van Lindley Nursery, excluding his personal property which was deeded to his wife (a plot of land 1170 x 300 feet, which equals about 8.1 acres), but moving about 1,130 acres into the company, the land being valued in the documents as being worth $30,000 (Guilford County Register of Deeds).

J. Van Lindley consolidated his properties into the "J. Van Lindley Nursery Company" on June 23, 1899. As part of a series of transactions, he extracted his personal home property and put it in the name of his wife, Sandia. The bulk of the rest of his property in Pomona, 1130 acres valued at $30,000, was moved into the newly formed corporation's name. J. Van had executed about 70 individual buy and sell transactions prior to that date and owned about 4000 acres, 1600 in Guilford County and 2400 in Moore County. An article in the Greensborough Patriot in 1899 states that the newly incorporated company owned: "...1250 acres two miles west of Greensboro." (Greensborough Patriot 4)

The reason for the incorporation may have had to do with J. Van's age or to improve his position for future business opportunities. J. Van was 61 years old by this time and his only son, Paul Cameron Lindley, was 22 years old. Paul attended Cornell University between 1895 and 1900, and was finishing up his studies as the company was incorporated (Cornell University).

Development of Land, Sale of Subdivision and Commercial Lots

The idea of suburban neighborhoods came about almost overnight with the new transportation improvements. First the trolley, and later the motor vehicle, made it possible for people to live further away from factories, yet earn a living working there. While the average farmer or factory worker was earning this wage, the foresight and enterprise of J. Van Lindley and his father Joshua placed him in a position to profit greatly from hitherto unforeseen opportunities.

J. Van Lindley understood the concept of subdividing land from his orchard operations in Southern Pines. The land for his peach shipping operations in Southern Pines was purchased from the New England Mining Manufacturing and Estate Company, the developers of Southern Pines. J. Van had also bought 3 lots in 1887, not previously mentioned, in Douglas Subdivision in Greensboro. These were lots 11, 12 and 13 in square 9 near the corner of Oak/Bragg and Macon in Southeast Greensboro. Another lot was purchased in 1897 from the Greensboro Land and Improvement Company in Morehead

Subdivision, a .27-acre tract on Jackson Street, north of Spring Garden.

Park Place was the name of the first subdivision that J. Van Lindley began to develop. He purchased 143 acres of land in 1881 for $1050 from D.S. Rainey. In 1900 he sold 21.25 of these acres for $850. In March of 1903 he began selling mostly half, and some full acre lots for $400-600 per half acre. It is important to note for comparison purposes that the average wage in the United States in 1904 was about $400 for a year, so each lot sold was the equivalent of an average person's annual wage. After 58 transactions between 1903 and 1918, J. Van Lindley Nurseries was able to clear over $20,000 in profits. Two lots off of West Market Street, north of Park Place were sold for an additional $21,000 in profits between 1908 and 1910.

The West Lee Street Subdivision was the next development. Forty acres of land was purchased in the Pomona area, south of the railroad tracks and immediately west of the location today of the Greensboro Coliseum. This rectangular tract was subdivided into lots of one-third, one-half and full acre lots. The sales for this subdivision went quickly and J. Van Lindley Nurseries were able to receive back $10,900 dollars on their $6,000 investment for a profit of just under $5,000.

Perhaps the most intently focused area of land purchases was along the North Carolina Railroad tracks in the Pomona area, including the junction that leads towards Winston-Salem. Along this corridor, following the dreams and vision laid down by his father, J. Van purchased just over 620 acres of land between 1878 and 1890 for a total purchase price of about $9,100.

By the time of his death in 1918, the J. Van Lindley Nurseries still owned about 600 acres at a net purchase price of about $7,600. On May 8, 1927 the Southern Railway company purchased 11.5 acres along the railroad tracks from J. Van Lindley Nurseries for $100,000.

Some of the remaining 550 acres of land along the railroad tracks included where J. Van Lindley and his family lived north of the tracks and on the south side of Spring Garden Street. Their home was beside the small office and shipping facilities facing the railroad track. J. Van's son Paul lived beside him before selling his property to his sister Pearl Lindley Sykes and her husband Archie. The Hunt family lived next to them and then the Boren family. The Lindley, Sykes, Hunt and Boren families were all related by marriage.

J. Van Lindley gradually sold off parcels and lots that lay next to Spring Garden and the railroad tracks between 1902 and 1918. Many of the purchasers worked for him in one of his enterprises. He netted an additional $5000 from these purchases, selling a total of about 29 acres, with the purchase price for these acres included in the railroad land purchases previously mentioned.

Muir's Chapel Road on the western side of Pomona was another concentrated area for J. Van Lindley's land purchases. He bought and sold land along this road from 1876 until his death. He owned as much as 770 acres in 1898, at a cumulative cost of $9,500 up to that point. His subsequent sales in this area included some lots developed along "First Street" (the precise location never confirmed on historical or current maps) and sales of land to Pomona Mills. The cumulative sales price for acreage in this area added up to $22,000 and a net profit of just under $12,500; plus, there was still 500 acres of land owned by the J. Van Lindley Nurseries at the time of his death.

The land in Southern Pines was purchased between 1891 through 1895 and totaled about 1700 acres for a cumulative cost of about $4,000, or about $2.50 per acre. The low cost of the land was because the ability to develop the land was not well understood. Thanks to the efforts of J. Van Lindley, the value of the land increased once it was demonstrated that peaches could be profitably grown on this land. The sale of 1100 acres in 1918 attests to this fact as the J. Van Lindley Orchard Company received $10,000, or about $9.06 per acre for the land. The records were not clear enough on the remaining acres to determine if much more was made on the remaining land than the $110 recorded in the sale of the deeds.

J. Van Lindley and the J. Van Lindley Nurseries also lent about 30 times between 1887 and 1911 in varying amounts from $100 to $2500 to help facilitate land purchases. The loans were always secured by land and were usually paid off within a few years. In the absence of readily available banking institutions and mortgage lenders, this may have been an economic necessity. After 1911, land sales continued without the need for J. Van Lindley to provide the financing.

Several additional developments of land owned by J. Van Lindley Nurseries included Lindley Park, land surrounding The Masonic Home, and Highland Park West (a small subdivision of streets named for Ivy League schools). These developments were more the work of Paul Cameron Lindley and his son John Van (Jack) Lindley.

Summarizing over 300 land transactions covering a 55-year period of activity, J. Van Lindley was able to generate at least $180,000 in profits during a time period when the average worker earned about $400 - $1,100 annually. Today's 2010 relative figures would have to multiplied by about 40 (the average wage today is about $46,000) to yield over $7 million in profits from his land development activities. This does not include the eventual profits from the 500+ acres owned in Greensboro at the time of his death or the 1000 acres owned in Harnett County; which will be explained later in this book.

J. Van Lindley

Figure 19 - J. Van Lindley

1905 - 1918: Industrialist, Philanthropist

The last 13 years of J. Van Lindley's life were probably his most fulfilling. He had already made many significant accomplishments and accumulated significant wealth. His desire to continue to achieve and take full advantage of the expanding opportunities led him to experiment with banking, insurance and cotton mill ventures. His cotton mill experience only lasted for a few years as a director of the Pomona Cotton Mill. He set up a bank in Kernersville, but closed it down when he moved his nearby nursery operations to Harnett County. The enduring member of these three ventures was the insurance company.

J. Van Lindley became concerned after the turn of the 20th Century that Southerners were sending their insurance premiums to Northern businesses that did not reinvest the profits in the local economy. In an attempt to establish a business that kept the profits within the South, J. Van Lindley started several insurance companies. He was President of the Underwriters Fire Insurance Company of Greensboro, the Southern Stock Mutual Fire Insurance Company, and the Security Life and Annuity Company of Greensboro. He was also a Director of the Southern Life and Trust Company, the Home Fire Insurance Company, and Southern Underwriters Fire Insurance Company.

While most of these above named enterprises did not last more than a few years, there was one significant exception. In 1912, as President of Security Life and Annuity Company of Greensboro, J. Van Lindley agreed to the merge with Jefferson Standard Life Insurance Company. J. Van Lindley became Vice President of the combined company and a major shareholder. Two of his son-in-laws, Dr. Joseph Turner and Clarence Leak, served as Vice-Presidents of the new company for the remainder of their working lives.

In 1913 J. Van attended the Northern Nut Growers Association's fourth annual meeting in Washington, DC on November 18th and 19th. He represented North Carolina along with Professor W.N. Hutt, the State Horticulturist. He is listed as being a member in the annual meeting minutes through 1917.

During this time period he continued to expand the small empire, which he had created into solid, sustainable businesses. He was able to see his son, Paul Cameron Lindley, and his sons-in-law, Archie Sykes, Joseph Turner, and Clarence Leak become much more involved in the management of his business interests during this time frame. Paul and Archie managed the J. Van Lindley nurseries, with Archie eventually being directly responsible for the florist business and Paul for the remainder. Paul, Joe, and Clarence were all involved in Jefferson Standard, with the latter two being Vice-Presidents at the company.

Kernersville, then Overhills

The land that J. Van Lindley Nurseries was developing and selling in Pomona needed to be replaced so his nursery business could continue to thrive. The initial answer was found in land west of Greensboro, in Forsyth County near Kernersville, NC. The land was along the railroad line that led to Winston-Salem.

Beginning in 1903, the J. Van Lindley Nurseries purchased 289 acres, then gradually added more land until there were 364 acres in 1907 and finally 500 acres in 1910. The new "growing fields" operation successfully kept up with business demand and the company learned how to operate using a remote location with an on-site manager named Atlas Simpson Davis.

In 1911 Paul Cameron Lindley became interested in land owned by the Kent-Jordon partnership in Harnett County. Paul was in his early 30's and J. Van was in his early 70's, so the transition in leadership at the company was beginning to occur. James Francis Jordon was a Greensboro native whose partnership with California Congressman William Kent had acquired 35,000 acres of land in Harnett and neighboring Cumberland Counties. They formed the Overhills Country Club and built roads, trails, stocked fishing ponds, stables and kennels for fox hunting, and a large clubhouse.

Paul visited and his interest lay not in the country club, but in the bottomlands along Jumping Run Creek. His subsequent purchase of these lands for J. Van Lindley Nurseries made the front page of the Fayetteville Observer on Wednesday, August 30, 1911. The article explained the events leading up to the purchase, along with his intentions for the land:

> "... A news reporter sought Paul C. Lindley, who returned from that section on Friday night, for more particulars of the deal. With Mr. Lindley was found James F. Jordan and Lewis H. Wise, practical forester, soil specialist and landscape designer of New York. They just returned from Harnett County, and when seen were looking over the conveyances passed between the parties on Thursday.
>
> What was learned from these gentlemen not only partly confirms a report of a land purchase by the Lindley Nursery Company but also relates to a wonderful development of Harnett County in the way of improved farming, the building of a model town...
>
> Mr. Lindley talked of his connection with the matter frankly, interestingly. When shown the news item published, he said: "the information is slightly misleading in that we bought the land from the Kent-Jordan company, and it lies in Harnett County, but we bought it not to plant apple orchards, but to raise nursery stock for apples, pecans, mulberries, ornamental trees, shrubs and plants. Our purchase is a mile square or about 700 acres... for some time we've been looking for rich black lands to raise stock and ship it to Greensboro houses, soil in which to grow plants in the greenhouses."
>
> "Speaking of this several months ago, Mr. Jordan invited me to pay a visit to this property as a guest and also as an investor. I was much pleased with what I saw, but was not sure the soil was what I needed, though the location and other natural ad-

vantages were satisfactory. To make sure, we sent
to New York for an expert scientist on soil, trees,
disease, etc., and Louis Wise came out. We spent
10 days in a careful and exhaustive test of soils,
etc., suitable for such purposes, and upon receiving Mr. Wise's report we closed the deal. Mr. Wise
in his report said that not only had he found the
soil suitable for our purposes but that upon comparison he found it equal, if not superior, to the
best nursery black soil of Michigan, recognized as
some of the finest in the world.

We will discontinue our branch nursery at Kernersville, in Forsyth County, and will dispose of that
holding of 500 acres and transfer all this work to
the Kent-Jordan purchase in Harnett. We will ship
12 mules there next weekend to begin plowing, and
a large force of men will at once be put to work
ditching, tilling and getting the ground in thorough tilth for next spring's planting. We will also
begin at once shipping this black dirt to Greensboro for greenhouses for plant and flower growth"
(Fayetteville Observer).

Figure 20 - Overhills, NC two-year-old Apple Trees

The 643.20 acres of land were purchased on September 1, 1911 for $16,000, with payments being made over a 5-year period. Atlas Simpson Davis moved to Harnett County to head up the operation and prepare the growing fields. As the fields were worked, a residence was constructed for Mr. Davis, along with three houses between his house and the bottomlands and another three houses on the ridge above the bottom for a total of seven homes for Mr. Davis's family and the families of the field workers. The Overhills Freight Station was built for shipping the stock to Greensboro and directly to customers. Paul Cameron Lindley had a story-and-a-half frame bungalow built as his residence for his trips to Overhills. He and his family also spent many holidays at this home.

The company purchased more acreage in 1914 to bring the total land holdings in Harnett County to 999.5 acres. The second purchase included a re-financing with a total of $15,000 borrowed by the nurseries from Jefferson Standard Life Insurance Company. After J. Van Lindley's death in 1918, Paul purchased an additional 225 acres in Harnett County.

In 1927, several frequent guests at the Country Club, led by Percy Rockefeller and Averill Harriman, founded the Overhills Land Company and purchased the estate. It was a world-renowned location in the 1920's and was particularly known for the premier polo facilities and for fox hunting.

The Great Depression brought an end to large-scale sporting events and also had an impact on the Lindley family. Overhills was bought by the Rockefellers as a private retreat and Isabella Rockefeller purchased the land owned by the J. Van Lindley Nurseries on February 24, 1932 for an undisclosed sum. At the same time, the $15,000 loan owed by the nurseries to Jefferson Standard was repaid, so her purchase price may have been (due to the financial pressures of the depression) only the sum necessary to remove the debt obligation.

Additional Association and Business Activities

The Piedmont North Carolina Immigration Association was created on January 11, 1906, at a meeting at the Benbow Hotel. J. Van Lindley was elected president. At the suggestion of T. K. Bruner, North Carolina Agriculture Secretary, the group proposed to send an agent to other countries to recruit immigrants to come directly to North Carolina, landing at Wilmington or Norfolk and bypassing Ellis Island. The rapid industrial expansion was creating a shortage of workers, especially in the agriculture and horticulture fields, and so the state was looking for a more direct supply of labor.

Despite the expansion of his business interests and responsibilities, J. Van Lindley remained attentive to his nursery stock, taking time to inspect it regularly and take quick action, if necessary, as described in the following account:

> Sometime in the summer of 1913 J. Van Lindley, owner of a tree farm and nursery near the Piedmont town of Pomona (not far from Greensboro in Guilford County) noticed curious yellow-orange blisters on some imported Japanese chestnut trees. Immediately concerned, the nurseryman conducted a hasty inspection of a few wild American chestnuts growing in the nearby woods. A

quick look confirmed his worst fears. Some of those trees, too, exhibited the telltale spots and cankers. Panicked, Van Lindley contacted John Simcox Holmes at the Geological Survey.

When the state forester heard the news, he promptly instructed the nurseryman to cut down, dig up, and incinerate every infected chestnut, Japanese and American alike, and clean and burn the ground on which the trees grew. Van Lindley complied, and a few months later, after state inspectors found no spots on the remaining trees, Holmes breathed a cautious sigh of relief. Perhaps, he thought, North Carolina had survived its first encounter with chestnut blight.

J. Van Lindley served on the Board of Directors of many businesses, the Board of Education, and remained President of the N.C. Horticulture Society during this time period:

Director of:

Southern Life And Trust Company
American Exchange National Bank
Van Story Clothing Company
Gate City Furniture Company
Greensboro Table And Mantle Company
Odell Hardware Company
Southern Stock Mutual Fire Insurance Co.
Mt. Airy Granite Company (NC Granite Corporation)
Home Fire Insurance Co.
Southern Underwriters Fire Insurance Co.
Pomona Cotton Mill Company

Member of:

Guilford County Board of Education in 1915

President of:

State Horticulture Society (until 1917)

Final Donation and Death

J. Van Lindley made a gift of sixty acres of wooded land near Pomona in May of 1918, which the Greensboro Record commented on with a tribute to his life:

> There is no form of philanthropy more far-sighted and productive of lasting good than the gift of a beautiful park of such proportions as to meet the needs of a city which someday will include in its boundaries not only the park but the fields and woods surrounding it.
>
> Greensboro is today the proud recipient of such a gift from a man whose life work has been the development of beautiful things not made with hands...It means that a beautiful residential section will be built up around it and attractive homes will be multiplied.
>
> This is Lindley Day in Greensboro where, by reason of his munificence, the name will live in grateful memory throughout the ages (Greensboro Record).

John Van Mons Lindley died on June 13, 1818 at the age of eighty.

Summary

The J. Van Lindley Nursery Company Board of Directors wrote into its minutes a eulogy to describe the man they knew so well, and it answers many of the questions posed in the prelude of this book:

> A lover of plants and flowers and trees he was nonetheless a lover of his fellow men. Whenever it was possible to assist a struggling young fellow to his feet and give him standing room to use his powers Mr. Lindley was quick to reach to him a friendly hand. His interests were broad and many. No effort looking toward the improvement of his community or state failed to receive his sympathy and support, whether this was for material advancement, as good roads, or for the mental and spiritual influence of the young in providing good schools, all met his encouragement and assistance. It was never enough for him to build up his own business and add field to field and amass wealth for himself. He looked beyond these things and labored for the general good and the up-building of a civilization founded upon righteousness.

A fuller description of the impact of his legacy on financial institutions, professional associations, community groups, educational institutions, nursery and manufacturing businesses, introductions of fruit, and descendent family members follows.

Financial Institutions

Jefferson-Pilot Life Insurance Company

In 1912, Jefferson Standard Life Insurance merged with Security Life and Annuity Company of Greensboro, of which J. Van Lindley was President. The company also merged at the same time with Greensboro Life Insurance Company and moved its headquarters from Raleigh to Greensboro. J. Van Lindley was made Vice President, a position he maintained until his death. Many of J. Van's descendants spent their professional lives working for the company. In April of 2005, Lincoln Financial bought Jefferson-Pilot. There is still one great-great-grandson working for the company - Jonathan Dickerson Stovall.

Security National Bank, NCNB, and Bank of America

The only two commercial banks in Greensboro shut their doors in quick succession in February and March of 1933. Five months later, Jefferson Standard started the Security National Bank with $750,000 of capital to provide banking services for the people and businesses of Greensboro. (Lamb) In 1945, Jefferson Standard merged with Pilot Life, who had banking interests as well. That put them in charge of two banks - Security National Bank and Guilford National Bank. The combination of these two banks meant that by 1950 Security National had a controlling interest in the Greensboro market, but was only modestly expanding beyond the city. J. Van Lindley's grandson, who shared the same name but went by his nickname "Jack," managed to negotiate a bank merger in 1960, which led to the creation of North Carolina National Bank (NCNB). NCNB became an aggressive acquirer of banks following the merger and, many mergers later, in 1998 bought and then became what is known today as Bank of America.

Professional Associations

American Association of Nurserymen

The American Association of Nurserymen began representing the industry in 1875. J. Van Lindley served as their First Vice President in 1891 and as their President in 1892, during their 16th and 17th years, respectively. He also served as the Vice President from North Carolina in the preceding and succeeding years.

Now in its 132nd year, the organization is named the American Nursery & Landscape Association (ANLA). It is the national voice of the nursery and landscape industry. Members grow, distribute, and retail plants of all types, and design and install landscapes for residential and commercial customers. ANLA provides education, research, public relations, and representation services to members (American Nursery & Landscape Association).

NC Horticulture Society and NC State Dept. of Plant Biology

The North Carolina Horticulture Society had its own fair, but its historical importance lay more in setting up the first Agricultural Experiment Station outside of Raleigh. While the Experiment Station was curtailed due to state level politics in 1898, it provided a model for how state, university and business interests could work together to solve horticulture challenges. Botany plant research began with the start of NC State University in 1887 with the appointment of Michael Gerald McCarthy, who was the researcher that worked so closely with J. Van Lindley.

Agricultural Society and State Fair of North Carolina

This was a powerful group beginning in 1852 and running through 1925. J. Van Lindley served on the Executive Committee. Their main function was to organize and run the State Fair.

The State Fair began in 1853 and, although taken over by the State of North Carolina in 1928, continues to operate 156 years after its start (NCpedia).

Guilford County Good Roads Association

The Good Roads Association, which Guilford County participated in, was formed by J. Van Lindley in 1902 as North Carolina's chapter of the National Highway Association. The association actively worked towards the establishment of a highway system in North Carolina with great success. The state spent $65 million to make 5,500 miles of roads. The work of the Good Roads Association led to the creation of the State Highway Commission in 1921, and in 1971, the State Highway Commission became the NC Department of Transportation. J. Van Lindley's grandson Jack was appointed to the State Highway Commission in the 1950's.

American Pomological Society

J. Van Lindley's father Joshua was one of the founders of the American Pomological Society (APS). J. Van took up his father's participation, serving as a Vice President representing North Carolina. J. Van was recognized as an enthusiastic expert on the southern commercial peach culture and was a pioneer in the commercial peach orchard business in the Sand Hill region of North Carolina. In a biography included in their publications at J. Van Lindley's death in 1918, the APS credited the commercial successes of the peach orchard industry in the Sand Hill area largely to J. Van Lindley's efforts (The American Pomological Society).

Southern Nurserymen's Association

J. Van Lindley was president of the Southern Nurserymen's Association in 1902. The Southern Nurserymen's Association changed its name to the Southern Nursery Association (SNA) and is still in existence. As a regional association, the SNA today works to advance the horticultural industry in the southeast by supporting and enhancing educational, commercial and research opportunities; by gathering, analyzing and disseminating information; and by providing a marketplace to promote the exchange and sale of nursery stock and other allied products to their members, participating state associations and the industry (Southern Nursery Association).

Community Benefactor

Children's Home Society

The Children's Home Society (CHS) was founded in 1902 by a group of visionary and compassionate businessmen, the Young Businessmen's Club of Greensboro (today the Chamber of Commerce) who were moved to address the issue of homeless children. The founders, whose names are still known today - Gold, Osborne, McIver, Duke, Lindley, Broughton, Hanes, Richardson, Douglas, Cone, Daniels, Battle and others - provided the stability and integrity that has guided the Society to this day.

Most of the children placed with families in the early years of CHS were older, between the ages of 4 and 12. Because CHS did not have a receiving home for children, they were often cared for in the homes of board members until a suitable family could be found. The pattern of placing older children continued through the 1920s.

With the advent of safe baby formula and the post World War II baby boom, CHS began placing more infants for adoption. From 1930 through the 1970s, the primary goal of CHS was to find homes for newborns. During these years, CHS began serving the entire state with offices emerging in seven cities.

Today, CHS provides a myriad of services beginning with counseling for birth mothers who are considering adoption and continuing as a resource for families long after their adoptions are final. To better serve the varied population, programs include Birth Parent Services, Foster Care, Adoption, and Therapeutic/Post Adoption Support (Children's Home Society).

Central Carolina Fair

J. Van Lindley was instrumental in the formation of the Central Carolina Fair and was President in the early years. The Central Carolina Fair has run continuously for over 100 years and survives to this date (Central Carolina Fair).

Figure 21 – J. Van Lindley Nursery's Arboretum

Lindley Park - Greensboro Arboretum

The Greensboro Arboretum is a 17-acre site that features 12 permanent plant collections and special display gardens, structural features including a fountain, overlook, arbor, gazebo, bridges and benches. Although created years after his death, it is actually a successor to the Lindley Arboretum used for exhibition plantings. The Greensboro Arboretum features nine permanent plant collections and a number of special garden areas and structural features. It is easily accessible to the public using an open, popular and stunningly beautiful walkway.

While created and maintained by the Greensboro Parks & Recreation Department (which dates its history back to J. Van Lindley's son Paul who started the first Camp and Playground Association in the 1920's) and Greensboro Beautiful, it would probably have been considered by J. Van Lindley to be a most fitting tribute to his love and lifelong devotion to horticultural beauty (Greensboro Beautiful).

Lindley Park Amusement Park and Neighborhood

Lindley Park and the neighborhood with the same label were named after J. Van Lindley. In 1902, he donated 60 acres of land along Spring Garden Street for a recreation complex boasting a man-made lake and amusement park (including 17 acres later used to create an arboretum). When the lake and amusement park closed in 1917, the City hired Earle Sumner Draper to design a planned neighborhood development. What followed was the Lindley Park neighborhood. Many original design elements still remain, such as the stone column entry-ways and tree-lined streets. The park area continues to exist today between Spring Garden Street and Walker Avenue and includes the City's Arboretum (City of Greensboro).

Lindley Park Recreation Center

The Lindley Recreation Center in Greensboro, NC is a facility that provides meeting rooms, multi-purpose rooms, a kitchen, gym and game area for community activities like sports, group meetings, association meetings, dances, and after school programs to support the community. The grounds include a public, Olympic-size swimming pool and grounds for additional activities (City of Greensboro).

Educational Institutions

J. Van Lindley Elementary and Junior High School

In 1877 J. Van Lindley built a school for the Pomona Community on Spring Garden Street adjacent to his nursery. This small school was replaced by a larger building in 1905, located to the east of the present school, and was used by the elementary students until it burned in 1933. A new school was built to replace it and J. Van Lindley Elementary today serves a diverse population of 458 students in Grades Kindergarten through Fifth Grade in Greensboro, NC as part of the Guilford County Public School System. The school has been in continuous existence for over 100 years serving its local community.

J. Van Lindley was credited as the founder of the Pomona High School, although it was not built until after his death. In 1920 the Pomona High School was built and in 1929 the name changed to the Lindley Junior High School in honor of J. Van Lindley. Lindley Junior High School is no longer in use, but is a Greensboro, NC Historic Landmark, listed as Pomona High School, and has recently been converted to student housing for neighboring University of North Carolina Greensboro students.

Guilford College

By the 1830s the majority of Quakers in North Carolina lived in and around Guilford County. They decided to establish a school on a coeducational basis that was chartered in 1834 and opened in 1837 as New Garden Boarding School. The campus later became a station on the Underground Railroad as well as a center of resistance to Confederate conscription and requisitioning efforts. Unlike other southern educational institutions, the school never closed during the Civil War. During Reconstruction, with support from Friends in the North and Great Britain, it quickly recouped its strength.

The boarding school subsequently set a course towards and eventually became Guilford College, the fourth oldest degree-granting institution in North Carolina. The college remained largely isolated until the 1920s, when the old trail to Greensboro became the Friendly Road. The street name still symbolizes the longstanding friendship between the town and the college. Today the campus is an area of greenery, quiet and scholarship within Greensboro's city limits. It is one of the very few college campuses in the nation listed by the United States Department of the Interior as a National Historic District, which still utilizes the buildings that J. Van Lindley was so keen to build: King Hall (rebuilt in 1908 due to a fire), Cox Hall and the Library (completed in 1909) (Thorne).

Nursery and Manufacturing Businesses

J. Van Lindley Nursery Company

Paul Cameron Lindley, who became the sole owner, following the death of his mother Sandia Lindley in 1926, changed the J. Van Lindley Nursery Company to Lindley Nurseries, Inc. The company continued to thrive until the Great Depression. Paul Lindley died by drowning in 1933 and J. Van "Jack" Lindley II became the company owner. As the depression continued, the Nursery business struggled, but survived.

Jack Lindley died many years later on October 20, 1990 with significant Lindley Nurseries, Inc. land holdings. Although his family expected a significant inheritance, the land holdings proved to be mortgaged with significant bank debt, enough that the company was essentially considered insolvent at that point.

Pinehurst-Southern Pines Orchard

The J. Van Lindley Orchard Company's properties spanned almost the entire area between present day Southern Pines and Pinehurst. The land was located on both sides of Midland Road, which connects the two towns. Several golf courses and their surrounding neighborhoods touch the roughly one mile square area:

- Midland Country Club

- Longleaf Golf & Country Club
- National Golf Club
- Mid South Club

Kernersville, NC & Overhills Nursery in Harnett County, NC

The Overhills Nursery bought by Isabella Rockefeller during the Great Depression from Paul Lindley was subsequently purchased by the U.S. Government and folded into land used by Fort Bragg for training. The land is not accessible any longer, but can be found on satellite maps. It is located east of route 24/87 on the north and west sides of Nursery Road, which makes a ninety-degree turn. The land includes the remains of about 28 buildings that were once used on the property including homes for the Superintendent, laborers and their families, Paul Lindley's cottage, along with sheds and packinghouses.

Town of Pomona, NC

In 1877, J. Van Lindley began working on his own as a sole proprietorship. He operated his business initially as Pomona Hills Nurseries, honoring Pomona, the ancient Roman goddess of fruit trees. In 1878 he acquired a tract of land, along Spring Garden Street and adjacent to the railroad tracks, just over 2 miles west of Greensboro. He bought the land from Joseph G. And Mary Hiatt and it formed the core site of his nursery business. Although the location was originally named Salem Junction Township, he had it changed to Pomona, NC. With additional purchases, he expanded to 1,130 acres in 1899 when he changed the business name to J. Van Lindley Nurseries (Guilford County Register of Deeds). The town of Pomona was gradually absorbed by the city of Greensboro as it expanded its city limits westward. Neighborhoods within the Pomona area that survive until today include the Lindley Park Neighborhood, parts of the Masonic Home subdivision, and the Highland West subdivision.

Figure 22 - Pomona Terra Cotta 1951, inset 1886

Pomona Terra Cotta

The Pomona Terra-Cotta Works had a capacity of 250 railroad carloads in 1893 using its 150-horse power engine and boiler. Their trade rapidly increased, making their capacity inadequate, and they moved to a new site, building another, larger plant with 375 steam horse power and output of 600 cars per year in 1899. (Greensborough Patriot 4) A few years later they ramped up further, producing almost 1,400 railroad cars of manufactured product in 1905 (Ashe, Weeks and Van Noppen 226). By 1925, the production was listed as 3,000 carloads of product (Meeker 64). Pomona Terra-Cotta became one of the leading manufacturers of sewer pipe in the South and later produced conduit tile that was used throughout the country. It operated for almost 100 years. At its peak, the firm ran over 40 kilns at four manufacturing plants in Greensboro on the Winston Road (now West Market Street) employing more than 300 men (Meeker 86).

Pomona Cotton Mill

The Pomona Cotton Mill opened in 1897 and closed in the 1950's. The mill initially appeared to prosper as it expanded, but financial tragedy struck in 1908. Creditors forced the company into bankruptcy after unwise investments resulted in a major financial loss. Pomona went into receivership, and their workers scattered in all directions in search of jobs in other mills. Debts were eventually settled, and the mill reopened as Pomona Mills, Inc.

By 1920, Pomona Mills, Inc. was prospering. A $400,000 addition was completed for dyeing and finishing, and 150 new looms were installed. The efficiency of the workers was attributed to the working conditions at the mill, described as among the best, and Pomona had a reputation for manufacturing the best corduroys, corset cloth and romper cloth on the market. The mill continued to prosper during World War II, but when the war was over, the mill operated only three or four days a week. Business continued its decline during the remainder of the 1940's. When the mill closed in 1950, a real estate firm from Winston-Salem handled the sale of the mill houses, giving employees the first chance to buy the houses they lived in (Koehler).

Piedmont Triad International Airport (formerly Lindley Field)

J. Van Lindley's son Paul sold land in Pomona and moved Lindley Nurseries further west to the township of Friendship due to the encroachment of the city of Greensboro. Greensboro and Guilford County jointly purchased the Friendship property from Paul C. and Helen G. Lindley, and christened it Lindley Field in May 1927 with 12,000 people in attendance. No runways, no lights, no hangar, and no passenger station existed at the time. Charles Lindbergh stopped at Lindley Field with the "Spirit of St. Louis" on his cross-country tour celebrating the advances of aviation on October 14, 1927. Regular mail service was established in 1928. The airport was renamed and expanded over the years and today is known as Piedmont Triad International Airport.

Introductions of Fruits

Summer Banana Apple

Figure 23 - Summer Banana Apple

This apple is from Marion County, South Carolina and was first grown in the late 1800's and trademarked by J. Van Lindley in 1900. It is so named because it can have a slight banana aroma when fully ripe. It is an apple with a finely grained flesh and is the best apple for frying. Its fresh taste is also quite exceptional for an apple ripening during the heat of the summer. The Summer Banana's fruit is usually medium in size, with a deep yellow, small light green splotches and perhaps a few red dots at its peak of ripeness. The fruit ripens beginning in August into September.

Conkleton Pear

The Conkleton Pear is described in "The Orchard, Lawn and Garden Guide" in the "Fruits for the South" section of the book where the author, George H. Reed, excerpted the entire section directly from the J. Van Lindley Company catalog with the following comment:

> "Published by permission of the J. Van Lindley Nursery Co., Pomona, N.C. 'Fruits for the South' is so well written that I consider it of high value to this book."

The Conkleton Pear, originally grown by J. Van Lindley, is included under the heading "Oriental Strain of Pears" and includes the following comments: "The most reliable class of Pears for the South. Good growers and productive."

There are two pears within this group, and since the Conkleton's description relies on understanding the Le Conte, both are included:

> "Conkleton. From Texas. Similar to its parent, Le Conte, but hardier in tree. A young and prolific bearer. Fruit size of Le Conte; better in quality, firmer in texture; a fine shipper.
>
> Le Conte. Fruit large and fair quality. Young and very prolific bearer; tree very hardy. Its beautiful fruit and foliage make it decidedly ornamental as well. September. (Reed, 1921, p. 81)"

James Grape

Figure 24 - James Grape

The James Grape was originated and introduced by J. Van Lindley of North Carolina. Like all varieties of this class, the vine is vigorous and perfectly healthy. The cluster is the largest and most prolific of any pure blood of the species. It contains 8 to 15 berries which are large, black, and round. The skin is thick, with pulpy flesh, exhibiting fair quality, and a musky smell. The seeds are large. They begin ripening at Denison, Texas about August 10th and continue for a month, then drop when ripe like all others of the species (Muson). The berries are probably the

largest variety of the southern muscadine type of grape, frequently measuring 1 ¼ inches in diameter (Reed 100-101).

Family Members

Paul Cameron Lindley

Paul C. Lindley was the only son of J. Van Lindley, and
followed in his father's footsteps as the majority owner of Lindley Nurseries. He also served as the Mayor of Greensboro from
1931 to 1933.

Dr. Joseph Pickney Turner

Dr. Turner was the husband of J. Van Lindley's oldest
daughter Eva. Dr. Turner was a Vice President at Jefferson
Standard Life Insurance.

Archie Jasper Sykes

Archie Sykes was the husband of J. Van Lindley's second
oldest daughter Pearl. Archie managed and then bought the
florist business on 115 S. Elm Street in 1925.

Clarence Leak

Clarence Leak was the husband of J. Van Lindley's third
oldest daughter Cammie. Clarence was a Vice President at
Jefferson Standard Life Insurance.

William Lanier Hunt

William Lanier Hunt, who grew up next door to J. Van
Lindley and was related through J. Van's wife's mother's family,
was a well known writer, landscape architect, and, in the early
days, a salesman for J. Van Lindley Nurseries. He wrote a book
titled Southern Gardens, Southern Gardening (1982) and was
well known at the University of North Carolina in Chapel Hill,

which houses his 400 boxes of personal papers in their Southern Historical Collection.

Index

Bibliography

1756 Will of Simon Hadley. (n.d.). Retrieved October 11, 2010, from The Hadley Society: //www.hadleysociety.org/photo_gallery/documents_gallery/index515.html

(1904, January). *Good Roads Magazine , V* (No. 1).

Albright, J. W. (1904). *Greensboro 1808-1904, Facts, Figures, Traditions and Reminiscences.* Greensboro: Jos. J. Stone & Company.

American Association of Nurserymen. (1892). *Proceedings, annual convention American Association of Nurserymen* (Vols. 17-19). Atlanta, GA: American Association of Nurserymen.

American Nursery & Landscape Association. (n.d.). *Our Organization.* Retrieved October 18, 2010, from http://www.anla.org/index.cfm?area=&page=Content&categoryID=91

Arnett, E. S. (1975). *Greensboro, North Carolina.* Chapel Hill, NC: University of North Carolina Press.

Ashe, S. A. (1925). David Fanning. In *Biographical History of North Carolina* (Vol. V). Greensboro, NC: C.L. Van Noppen.

Ashe, S., Weeks, S., & Van Noppen, C. L. (1905). *Biographical History of North Carolina from colonial Times to the Present* (Vol. 2). Greensboro, NC: Charles L. Van Noppen.

Backhouse, T. J., Backhouse, E., & Mounsey, T. (1854). Biographical Memoirs: being a record of the Christian Lives, Experiences and Deaths of members of the religious Society of Friends, from its rise to 1653. *I .* London, UK: W. and F.G. Cash.

Bailey, C. H. (n.d.). *Lindley and Allied Families, 1641-1946.* Retrieved from Ancestry.com.

Baker, M. A. (1991). John Van Lindley. In W. S. Powell, *Dictionary of North Carolina Biography* (Vols. 4, L-O, p. 67). Chapel Hill, NC: University of North Carolina Press.

Barefoot, D. W. (1998). *Touring North Carolina's Revolutionary sites.* Winston-Salem, NC: John F. Blair.

Bennett, W. D. (1989). *Orange County Records* (Vols. 2, Books 1&2). Raleigh, NC: William D. Bennett.

Biographical and Historical Record of Kosciusko County, Indiana. (1887). Chicago, IL: Lewis Publishing Co.

Blanchard, C. (1884). *Counties of Morgan, Monroe and Brown, Indiana: historical and biographical.* Chicago: F.A. Battey & Co.

Botkin, D. B. (2004). *Beyond the Stony Mountains: Nature in the American West from Lewis and Clark to Today.* New York, NY: Oxford University Press.

Branson & Farrar. (1866-1896). *Branson's North Carolina business directory, containing facts, figures, names and locations, revised and corrected annually.* Raleigh, NC: Branson & Farrar.

Bureau of Land Management. (n.d.). *Land Patent Search.* Retrieved October 12, 2010, from http://www.glorecords.blm.gov/PatentSearch/Default.asp?

Calhoon, R. M. (2003). Loyalism and neutrality. In J. P. Greene, & J. R. Pole, *A Companion to the American Revolution* (p. 235).

Carpenter, W. L., & Colvard, D. W. (1987). *Knowledge is Power, A History of the School of Agriculture and Life Sciences at North Carolina State University 1877-1984.* Raleigh, NC: North Carolina State University School of Agriculture and Life Sciences.

Caruthers, E. (1854). *Revolutionary Incidents and Sketches of Character Chiefly in the "Old North State".* Philadelphia: Hayes & Zell.

Central Carolina Fair. (n.d.). *Central Carolina Fair - Greensboro.* Retrieved October 18, 2010, from http://centralcarolinafair.com/default.html

Chester County, P. (n.d.). *Theresa Pogue files...from* <mannesah27@cox.net>, Linda Bucholz. Retrieved October 7, 2010, from www.genealogy.com: http://www.genealogy.com/users/p/o/g/Theresa-Pogue/FILE/0009text.txt

87

Joseph C. Carlin   187

Children's Home Society. (2002). Children's Home Society, 100 Year Anniversary. Greensboro, NC: Children's Home Society.

cited, A. O.-m. (n.d.). *John Isaac Lindley.* Retrieved October 7, 2010, from http://trees.ancestry.com/tree/16492581/person/384368149?ssrc=&ftm=1

City of Greensboro. (n.d.). *Lindley Park.* Retrieved October 18, 2010, from http://www.greensboro-nc.gov/departments/hcd/planning/neighplan/lindley.htm

Coffin, A. (1897). *Life and travels of Addison Coffin, written by Himself.* Retrieved from http://www.archive.org/details/lifetravelsofaddoocoff.

Cornell University. (1908). *The Ten-Year Book of Cronell University* (Vol. 4). Ithaca, NY.

Dictionary of American Family Names. Oxford University Press.

Dobbins, C. L. (2005, January 20). *Indiana Land Values and Cash Rent Update.* Retrieved November 23, 2010, from Purdue University Department of Agricultural Economics: http://www.agecon.purdue.edu/extension/prices/land/LandValue&CashRentUpdate05.pdf

Dobbs, G. R. (2006). *The Indian Trading Path and Colonial Settlement Development in the North Carolina Piedmont.* Chapel Hill: Gladys Rebecca Dobbs.

Dolan, J. (1972). *English Ancestral Names, The evolution of the Surname from Medieval Occupations.* New York: Clarkson N. Potter, Inc.

Dyer, F. H. (1908). *A Compendium of the War of the Rebellion* (Vol. 3). Des Moines, IA: The Dyer Publishing Company.

Emerson, C. (1886). *Chas. Emerson's North Carolina tobacco belt directory.* Greensboro, NC: Emerson.

Esarey, L. (Indianapolis). *A History of Indiana: From its exploration to 1850.* 1915: W.K. Stewart Co.l.

Fanning, C. D. (1861). *Narrative of Colonel David Fanning, written by himself, detailing astonishing events in North Carolina from 1775 to 1783.* Richmond, VA: Confederate States of America.

Fanny & Vera. (n.d.). *Fanny & Vera's Helpful Hints & Timely Tips for Civil War Reenactors.* Retrieved October 15, 2010, from http://www.shasta.com/suesgoodco/newcivilians/gents/mensovercoats.htm

Fayetteville Observer. (1911, August 30). p. 1.

Flick, W. (1904). *Transactions for the Year 1903.* Indianapolis, IN: Indiana Horticultural Society.

Futhey, J. S., & Cope, G. (1881). *History of Chester County, Pennsylvania: with genealogical and Biographical Sketches* (Vol. I). Philadelphia: Louis H. Everts.

Greensboro Beautiful. (n.d.). *The Gardens > The Arboretum within Lindley Park at Market Street & Starmount Drive.* Retrieved October 18, 2010, from http://www.greensborobeautiful.org/Arboretum.htm

Greensboro City. (1892). *Greensboro City Directory for 1892-93.* Greensboro, NC: Stone & Kendall.

Greensboro Record. (1918, May). Lindley Day in Greensboro. *Greensboro Record .*

Greensboro Times. (1856, January 21). "The Road Completed". *Greensboro Times* , p. 1.

Greensborough Patriot. (1899, May 3). Pomona Hills Nurseries and Pomona Terra Cotta Co. *Greensborough Patriot* , p. 4.

Guilford College. (1849-1856). Student Records for New Garden Boarding School.

Guilford County Register of Deeds. (n.d.). *Guilford County, NC Register of Deeds Online Records System.* Retrieved October 12, 2010, from http://rdlxweb.co.guilford.nc.us/guilfordNameSearch.php

Guilford County Register of Deeds. (n.d.). *Online Records System .* Retrieved October 18, 2010, from http://rdlxweb.co.guilford.nc.us/guilfordNameSearch.php

Hadley, W. H., Haorton, D. G., & Strowd, N. C. (1976). *Chatham County, 1771-1971.* Durham, NC: Moore Publishing Co.

Hairr, J. (2002). *Harnett County, A History*. Charleston, SC: Arcadia Publishing.

Henderson, A. (1941). *North Carolina, The Old North State and the New*. Chicago, IL: Lewis Publishing Co.

Hinshaw, W. W. (1969). *Encyclopedia of American Quaker Genealogy* (Vol. I). Baltimore: Genealogical Publishing Company.

Historical Society of Pennsylvania. *Records of Wicklow Monthly Meeting, Ireland*. Philadelphia, PA: Historical Society of Pennsylvania.

Hofmann, M. M. (1987). *The Granville District of North Carolina 1748-1763, Abstracts of Land Grants* (Vol. 2 and 3). Ahoskie, NC: Atlantic Printing.

Huntington County Historical Society. (1887). *History of Huntington County, Indiana*. Chicago, IL: Brant & Fuller.

Kilroy, P. (1994). *Protestant Dissent and Controversy in Ireland 1660-1714*. Ulster: University of Ulster.

Koehler, P. (2008, August 3). Old Mill Prospered Early in the 20th Centruy. *Greensboro News and Record* .

Lamb, D. (2009, December 22). *Greensboro Banks: History*. Retrieved November 23, 2010, from News & Record Research: http://nrtimelines.wetpaint.com/page/Greensboro+Banks:+History

Lefler, H., & Wager, P. (1953). *History of Orange County*. Chapel Hill, NC: The Orange Print Shop.

Lindley, H. (1916). *Indiana as seen by Early Travelers*. Indianapolis, IN: Indiana Historical Commission.

Lindley, J. (1853). Catalogue of Fruit Trees (From 1853 to 1856). New Garden, Guilford County, NC: North Carolina Pomological Garden and Nurseries.

Lindley, J. (1857). Catalogue of Fruit Trees (From 1857 to 1860). 3-5. Greensboro, NC: Joshua Lindley, Vice President of the American Pomological Congress.

Lindley, J. (1853). Catalogue of fruit trees, cultivated and for sale at the North-Carolina Pomological Garden and Nurseries from 1853 to 1856. Raleigh, NC: Star Office.

Lindley, J. M. (1924, 1930). *History of the Lindley, Lindsley, Linsley Families in America* (Vols. I - 1639-1930, II - 1639-1924). Winfield, IA.

Lindley, J. V. (n.d.). *NC State University Collections.* Retrieved October 18, 2010, from Letter from J. Van Lindley: http://repository.lib.ncsu.edu/collections/bitstream/1840.6/646/1/0001_Le tterfromJVanLindleyApril261901.pdf

Lindley, T. M. (n.d.). *Lindley Genealogy Page.* Retrieved October 7, 2010, from http://lindleyonline.com/lindley/genealogy.htm

McPherson Compton, B. E. (n.d.). *The Scots-Irish From Ulster and The Great Philadelphia Wagon Road.* Retrieved October 7, 2010, from http://www.electricscotland.com/history/america/wagon_road.htm

Meeker, M. J. (2004). *Enterprising Spirit.* Chapel Hill, NC: Chapel Hill Press.

Missouri Secretary of State. (n.d.). *Civil War Enlistment Document for John V. Lindley.* Retrieved October 15, 2010, from http://www.sos.mo.gov/TIF2PDFConsumer/DispPDF.aspx?fTiff=/archives/ AdjutantGerneral/Civil_War/ServiceCards/s838/0316.tif&Fln=S197092.pdf

Missouri's Civil War Heritage Foundation. (n.d.). *The Civil War in Missouri.* Retrieved October 15, 2010, from http://www.mocivilwar.org/history/1861.html

Moore County. (n.d.). Register of Deeds.

mrbuldog@sirius.com. (1998, Jul 7). JAMES LINDLEY II BIOGRAPHY.

Mudd, J. A. (1909/1992). *With Porter in North Missouri.* Iowa City, IA: Press of the Camp Pope Bookshop.

Mulcahy, M. (2009, January 17). *IrishTimes.com "Movers and Quakers".* Retrieved October 7, 2010, from http://www.irishtimes.com/newspaper/magazine/2009/0117/12320596542 86.html

Muson, T. (1909). *foundations of American Grape Culture*. New York, NY: Orange Judd Company.

Myers, A. C. (1902). *Immigration of the Irish Quakers into Pennsylvania 682-1750 with their early history in Ireland*. Retrieved October 7, 2010, from Google Books: http://books.google.com/books?id=7ZedLPs2fj0C&printsec=frontcover&dq =Immigration+of+the+Irish+Quakers&source=bl&ots=qQQaILfkiu&sig=jbb a_C3sDj6iAmwkYvlWBBpEz-w&hl=en&ei=WCOuTOqpJYOC8gbukp3- BA&sa=X&oi=book_result&ct=result&resnum=9&ved=0CDoQ6AEwCA#v= onepage

N.C. State Archives. (1881). Joshua Lindley Will. *Lindley, Joshua* . Raleigh, NC.

NC, Office of Secretary of State. (1766, September 22). File No. 0147, Thomas Lindley, Sr. *Land Office: Land Warrants, Plats of Survey, and Related Records - Orange County* .

NC, Office of Secretary of State. (1757, May 11). File No. 791, Thomas Lindley.

NC, Office of Secretary of State Granville Proprietary Land Office. (1756, February 3). Lindley, Thomas. Orange Co. *Land Office: Land Warrants, Plats of Survey, and Related Records - Orange County* .

NC, Office of Secretary of State. (1756, February 3). Lindley, Thomas. Orange Co. *Granville Proprietary Land Office: Land Entries, Warrants, and Plats of Survey* .

NCpedia. (2002). *The History of the State Fair*. Retrieved October 18, 2010, from http://ncpedia.org/government/fair/history

Newlin, A. I. (1984). *Friends "at the Spring:" a history of Spring Monthly Meeting*. Guilford, NC: Algie I. Newlin.

Newlin, A. I. (1975). *The Battle of Lindley's Mill*. Alamance Historical Association.

Newlin, A. I. (1965). *The Newlin Family Ancestors and Descendants of John and Mary Pyle Newlin*. Guilford, NC: Algie I. Newlin.

Newlin, H. (n.d.). *The Newlin Family*. Retrieved October 11, 2010, from The Family History and Genealogy of Laura and Elizabeth Henderson: http://www.laurahenderson.com/genealogy/genweb/ps01_045.html

Nichols, B. (2004). *Guerrilla Warfare in Civil War Missouri, 1862.* McFarland & Co.

North Carolina Highway Historical Marker Program, marker J-102. (n.d.). *5.2 The North Carolina Railroad.* Retrieved November 11, 2010, from Learn NC: http://www.learnnc.org/lp/editions/nchist-antebellum/4887

Ohio Pomological Society. (1859). *Transactions of the Ohio Pomological Society: Ninth Session, held at Columbus, December 7th to 9th, 1859...with an appendix: Memoirs of the Pioneer Frut Growers of the Ohio Valley.* Columbus, OH: Follett, Foster & Co.

Orange County NC Clerk of Court. (1780, March 15). Thomas Lindley, Sr. Will. *A* , 252. Hillsboro, NC.

Ragan, R. (1872). Joshua Lindley. *Transactions of the Indiana Horticultural Society* , *11*, p. 123.

Ragan, W. (1906). The First Indiana Horticultural Society. *Indiana Magazine of History* , *4*, p. 72.

Reck, M. P. (1983). *A History of the Piggott - Pickett Family, 1680-1983.* Sheridan, IN: M.P. Reck.

Reed, G. H. (1921). *The orchard, lawn and garden guide.* Lynchburg, Virginia: Brown-Morrison Co., Inc.

Ross, K. (n.d.). *Federal Militia in Missouri.* Retrieved October 15, 2010, from http://www.civilwarstlouis.com/militia/federalmilitia.htm

Salsi, L. a. (2002). *Guilford County, Heart of the Piedmont.* Charleston, SC: Arcadia Publishing.

Saunders, W. L. (1890). *The Colonial Records of North Carolina, 1769-1771* (Vol. 8). Raleigh, NC.

Savage, L. D. (n.d.). *The Anti-Salvery Friends in Salem.* Retrieved October 15, 2010, from http://www.icelandichorse.info/salemantislaveryfriends.html

Sheets, E. H. (1907). Baptists, the Regulators and Capt. Benjamin Merrill. In E. H. Sheets, *History of the Liberty Baptist Association* (p. 151). Raleigh, NC: Edwards & Broughton.

Smith, M. K. (n.d.). *Mary Kelly Watson Smith Diary Excerpts*. Retrieved November 19, 2010, from Greensboro Historical Museum: http://www.greensborohistory.org/archives/highlights/Smith_Diary/diary_ excerpts.htm

Southern Garden History Society. (1992, Summer/Fall). *IX, No. 1*.

Southern Nursery Association. (n.d.). *Past Presidents & Meeting Locations*. Retrieved October 18, 2010, from http://www.sna.org/pastpres.cfm

Stockard, S. (1902). *The History of Guilford County, North Carolina*. Knoxville, TN: Gaut-Ogden.

Taylor, W. A. (1902). *Promising New Fruits*. Washington, D.C.: Government Printing Office.

The American Pomological Society. (n.d.). *What is the American Pomological Society?* Retrieved October 18, 2010, from http://americanpomological.org/

The Greensborough Patriot. (1856, February 1). Finished! *The Greensborough Patriot* , p. 1.

Thomas, D. (1819). *Travels through the western country in the summer of 1816: including notices of the natural history, antiquities, topography, agriculture, commerce and manufactures; with a map of the Wabash country, now settling*. New York, NY: Auburn.

Thorne, D. L. (1937). *Guilford, A Quaker College*. Greensboro, NC: J.J. Stone & Company.

Tokyo Monthly Meeting. (n.d.). *Quaker Declaration of Pacifism*. Retrieved October 15, 2010, from http://www2.gol.com/users/quakers/quaker_declaration_of_pacifism.htm

Tottenham Quakers. (n.d.). *Dressed in Simplicity "Quaker record-keeping"*. Retrieved October 7, 2010, from http://www.tottenhamquakers.org.uk/history/Quakers006.html

Town of Mountmellick. (n.d.). *Welcome to Mountmellick "Arrival of the Quakers"*. Retrieved October 10, 2010, from http://www.mountmellick.net/history/quakers/arrivalofthequakers.htm

United States Government. (1860). *Eighth Census of the United States*. National Archives and Records Administration. Washington, D.C.: Census Bureau.

United States Government. (1930). *Fifteenth Census of the United States*. Washington, D.C.: Bureau of the Census.

United States Government. (1830). *Fifth Census of the United States*. Bureau of the Census. Washington D.C.: National Archives.

United States Government. (1790). *First Census of the United States*. National Archives. Washington, D.C.: Records of the Bureau of the Census.

United States Government. (1920). *Fourteenth Census of the United States*. National Archives and Records Administration. Washington, D.C.: Bureau of the Census.

United States Government. (1820). *Fourth Census of the United States*. Bureau of the Census. Washington, D.C.: National Archives.

United States Government. (1870). *Ninth Census of the United States*. Washington, D.C.: National Archives and Records Administration.

United States Government. (1800). *Second Census of the United States*. Washington, D.C.: Bureau of the Census.

United States Government. (1850). *Seventh Census of the United States*. Washington, D.C.: National Archives.

United States Government. (1840). *Sixth Census of the United States*. National Archives and Records Administration. Washington, D.C.: Bureau of the Census.

United States Government. (1880). *Tenth Census of the United States*. Washington, D.C.: National Archives and Records Administration.

United States Government. (1810). *Third Census of the United States*. National Archives. Washington, D.C.: Bureau of the Census.

United States Government. (1910). *Thirteenth Census of the United States*. National Archives and Records Administration. Washington, D.C.: Bureau of the Census.

United States Government. (1900). *Twelfth Census of the United States*. National Archives and Records Administration. Washington, D.C.: Bureau of the Census.

United States Record and Pension Office. (1902). *Organization and status of Missouri troops, Union and Confederate, in service during the Civil War*. Washington, DC: Government Printing Office.

United States War Department. (1880-1901). *The War of Rebellion: A Compilation of the Official Records of the Union and Confederate Armies, Series I* (Vol. XIII). Washington, D.C.: Government Printing Office.

University of Georgia Library. (n.d.). *Historical Broadsides 1880-1889*. Retrieved March 3, 2009, from http://fax.libs.uga.edu/bro/1f/historical_broadsides_1880_1889.pdf

Vann, R. T., & Eversley, D. (1992). *Friends in life and death, The British and Irish Quakers in the demographic transition, 1650-1900*. Cambridge, UK: Cambridge University Press.

Wallace, R. D., & Johnson, W. P. (1966). *North Carolina Genealogical Reference*. Durham, NC: The Seeman Printery, Inc.

Wallis, J. J. *The Property Tax as a Coordinating Device: Financing Indiana's Internal Improvement System, 1835 to 1842*. University of Maryland and National Bureau of Economic Research.

Warner, E. (1964). *Generals in Blue*. Baton Rouge, LA: Louisiana State University Press.

Weeks, E. B. *Register of Deeds, Orange County, NC, 1752-1768, and 1793*. Danielsville, GA: Heritage Papers.

Weeks, S. B. (1909). *Index to the colonial and state records of North Carolina covering volumes i-xxv*. Goldsboro, NC: Nash Brothers.

Wellman, M. W. (1974). *The story of Moore County: two centuries of a North Carolina region*. Southern Pines, NC: Moore County Historical Association.

Wikipedia. (n.d.). *Cane Creek Mountains*. Retrieved October 7, 2010, from http://en.wikipedia.org/wiki/Cane_Creek_Mountains

Wikipedia. (n.d.). *George Fox*. Retrieved October 7, 2010, from
http://en.wikipedia.org/wiki/George_Fox

Wikipedia. (n.d.). *Granville District*. Retrieved October 7, 2010, from
http://en.wikipedia.org/wiki/Granville_District

Wikipedia. (n.d.). *Land Act of 1820*. Retrieved October 12, 2010, from
http://en.wikipedia.org/wiki/Land_Act_of_1820

Wikipedia. (2009, November 10). *Lindley, West Yorkshire*. Retrieved
October 7, 2010, from Lindley, West Yorkshire:
http://en.wikipedia.org/wiki/Lindley,_West_Yorkshire

Wikipedia. (n.d.). *Quantrill's Raiders*. Retrieved October 15, 2010, from
http://en.wikipedia.org/wiki/Quantrill's_Raiders

Wikipedia. (n.d.). *War of the Regulation*. Retrieved October 11, 2010, from
http://en.wikipedia.org/wiki/War_of_the_Regulation

Wikipedia. (n.d.). *Westfield, Indiana and the Underground Railroad*.
Retrieved October 12, 2010, from
http://railroad.wikispaces.com/The+Underground+Railroad+in+Westfield,
+Indiana

Wilson, L. (n.d.). *Descendants of Joshua Lindley*. Retrieved October 12,
2010, from http://familytreemaker.genealogy.com/users/e/a/t/Linda-
wilson-Eaton-CA/GENE1-0001.html

Wylie, T. A. (1890). *Indiana University, its history from 1820, when
founded, to 1890*. Indianapolis, IN: William B. Burford.

About the Author

This is Joe Carlin's first published book. It has grown out of his love of family and interest in genealogy. The process of completing this writing has rekindled two of Joe's childhood interests: History and Literature.

Writing represents a radical career change for Joe. He has spent most of his life as a corporate finance executive working for IBM and Böwe, Bell, and Howell. After many years in the business world, Joe enjoys the solitude and intellectual challenge of a writer's life.

Joe plans to continue to write. His dream is to fill a shelf with books representing the physical product of his intellect and imagination.

CPSIA information can be obtained
at www.ICGtesting.com
Printed in the USA
FSOW04n2119081117
40955FS